The Times-Picayune

KATRINA

THE RUIN AND RECOVERY OF NEW ORLEANS

As the post-Katrina era entered its third month, the 17th Street Canal along the parish line divided a city of light, Jefferson Parish, from the darkness of Orleans Parish's obliterated Lakeview neighborhood.

Published by

The Times-Picayune

3800 Howard Ave.
New Orleans, LA 70125

Distributed by
Spotlight Press
Champaign, IL
www.spotlightpress.com

First printing, July 2006
Second printing, September 2006

ISBN - 13: 978-1-59670-184-7
ISBN - 10: 1-59670-184-6

Printed in Canada

About this book

The wavy brown line, where Lake Pontchartrain lapped against the house, streaks the weatherboards five feet above my head. Tiny, petrified frog carcasses are plastered to the walls. Inside, the mold reaches to the ceiling. I gaze at the ruined remnants of 16 years of family life – paperbacks swollen from immersion exploding their bookcase, slides from family trips blackened, Mardi Gras beads spilling out of the attic.

Six months after Hurricane Katrina, this is the house of my colleague James O'Byrne, features editor of The Times-Picayune, his wife and their two sons. I once sat in this living room while James introduced me to the magic of surround-sound. The centerpiece of his demonstration, a 51-inch Sony high definition projection TV, is still in place, defunct and coated in the salt water's silver residue.

You could walk out of this house and drive east past an uninterrupted succession of collapsed houses, gutted houses, houses no one has entered since August 29, 2005, houses that rose with the water and drifted down the block with their slabs attached, coming to rest in somebody's front yard. You could drive for two hours without ever leaving this lifeless zone, an urban devastation seven times the size of Manhattan. But you could also head six miles south, sip a Sazerac and slurp Oysters Rockefeller at Galatoire's in the heart of the French Quarter. Its elevated terrain, having escaped the flooding, is already abuzz with locals and tourists. In Katrinian New Orleans, topography is destiny.

Times-Picayune employees evacuate the newspaper plant as it is engulfed in floodwaters, a day after Hurricane Katrina.

When the floodwaters of Lake Pontchartrain burst through the federal government's shoddily built floodwalls and into our streets, the unthinkable occurred: An American city ravaged as no other in modern times, its urban landscape and human vibrancy drowned in acres of water and muck, its commerce choked off, its spirit almost suffocated. Our way of life and sense of order were wiped out in a day.

"NEW ORLEANS, A YEAR AFTER KATRINA, IS ON THE MEND. IT'S A FITFUL RECOVERY, AT ONCE DRAMATICALLY TRANSFORMATIVE AND TORTUROUSLY SLOW."

For us at The Times-Picayune, the catastrophe ushered in a story that will not end. Like New Orleanians from every walk of life, the newspaper's employees lost homes and cars and heirlooms in the flood. Likewise, the newspaper's offices suffered: Our suburban bureau in St. Bernard Parish was inundated, and our East Jefferson bureau was badly damaged. Water rose several feet around our headquarters building, making it unusable for six weeks.

Somehow, what might have been a crippling blow to staff morale and our very ability to function as a newspaper instead brought out our best, from the newsroom to the pressroom, from advertising to circulation. A team of photographers and reporters risked the chaos that had engulfed New Orleans and stayed behind to compile a vivid record. Meanwhile, the paper's editing, production and business functions were moved hastily to Baton Rouge, where we were taken in by LSU's Manship School of Mass Communication, as well as operating out of leased offices. Printing was arranged on borrowed presses, first at The Houma Courier and then at the Press-Register in Mobile.

It would be disingenuous to say that we can tell this story dispassionately. Nor should we. The journalists who covered Katrina and who wrote, illustrated and created this book are better chroniclers for having experienced the tragedy firsthand, for having seen the devastation in their own homes and neighborhoods. Though impassioned, they have never lost sight of the facts. They vigilantly debunked the myths and exaggerations about New Orleans after the storm. They investigated the causes of the levee failures, a civil engineering disgrace of historic dimension. And they have made themselves experts in explaining the complexity of our reordered world: how flood control structures are built and why they fail; how the coast of Louisiana is disappearing into the Gulf of Mexico and why every American should care; how to begin stitching together an urban fabric that has been ripped to shreds; how to cover a story that is about our own lives.

They have put their passion in the service of this extraordinary story.

New Orleans, a year after Katrina, is on the mend. It's a fitful recovery, at once dramatically transformative and torturously slow. We who live here are committed to rebuilding a historic city that is both a cultural treasure to the world and a vital commercial link for the United States; a city that appeals to the senses and extols the human scale of an urban community. We must love New Orleans back to life.

Jim Amoss

Jim Amoss, Editor, The Times-Picayune

CONTENTS

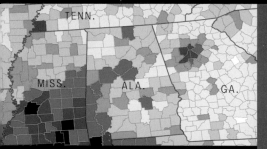
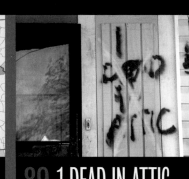

KATRINA DID NOT END WITH THE ARRIVAL OF AN ARMADA OF BUSES AND THE BELATED REMOVAL OF NEW ORLEANIANS WHO WERE TRAPPED IN THE HELLS THAT WERE THE SUPERDOME AND THE CONVENTION CENTER. It did not end in mid-October when the last of the floodwaters finally were pumped out of a city below sea level. It did not end with Mardi Gras or the temporary patch-ing of the failed federal levee system — though those events gave hope that Katrina might end one day, perhaps years from now. Katrina and the flooding it triggered were the worst engineering failure in the nation's history, a trauma costly both in dollars and the incalcu-lably more valuable currency of human life. This book is a visual

St. Paul's Episcopal Church in Lakeview, a muddied mess in Katrina's aftermath, was by late May the scene of the church school's eighth-grade graduation.

record of a ghastly hurricane and of the pregnant first months of the post-Katrina era. Already it is possible to see signs of progress and recovery. It is also possible, across vast swaths of the city, to see the persistence of a disaster that southeast Louisiana is struggling to survive.

Interstate 10, top, as stranded storm survivors thronged the buses, Sept. 3, 2005. The same location nine months later.

Sand heaved from the failed London Avenue Canal after the walls collapsed on Aug. 29, 2005. The same area in April 2006.

ake Pontchartrain's Mandeville shoreline as Rita approached in late September 2005, and as it appeared in early June 2006.

Old Spanish Trail in Slidell on the day Katrina struck — the boaters are Bob Smith, left, and Keith James — and in December 2005.

After Katrina, the window of a wrecked house framed the FEMA trailer that had become home to neighbors across the street. By late May 2006, the trailer remained in place, but the wrecked house had been knocked down and hauled away.

By June 2006, little progress could be detected at the site of this wrecked condo on Slidell's Lakeview Drive — except that the crushed pickup had been hauled away to reveal a crushed sedan behind it.

Two weeks after Katrina, putrid waters still overlay South Broad Street adjacent to the police complex and parish prison. By May, debris had been cleared and a semblance of normalcy achieved, though many buildings were still abandoned.

Top, the Lower 9th Ward as seen from above the breached Industrial Canal in mid-December. Bottom, the same area in early summer after shattered homes were bulldozed, the canal floodwall rebuilt and the barge cut up for scrap.

The Delta baggage claim area at Louis Armstrong International Airport was used as a triage center for the ill and the elderly as they were evacuated from New Orleans the weekend after the hurricane. Bottom, the same area nine months later.

The mud has dried and cracked, but in other respects the ruins of St. Rita's Nursing Home were eerily unchanged three months after the owners — later charged with negligent homicide — refused to evacuate the St. Bernard Parish facility and Katrina claimed the lives of 34 elderly residents.

CLOCKWISE FROM TOP LEFT: Miranda Truehill exhorts the faithful outside Mid-City's First United Baptist Church as Katrina closes in. • A Saturday night going-away party for Colorado-bound Rosalind Lobrano and Ryan Reboul turns into a hurricane party, a venerable New Orleans tradition. • Hunter Foret, 9, helps his family board up their home in the fishing village of Jean Lafitte. • Vanna White and Pat Sajak sup at Brennan's. • A Sunday afternoon bicyclist cruises emptying streets as New Orleans evacuates. • Lisa Barnett waits in a lengthening line as shoppers stock up at a supermarket in Covington. • The Saints stumble to a preseason loss against Baltimore, on the Friday before Katrina turned the Superdome into a seething shelter.

THE LAST WEEKEND

AUG. 28, 2005

AFTER CROSSING SOUTH FLORIDA, KATRINA LUMBERED INTO THE GULF LATE THURSDAY AND NEW ORLEANS REVERTED TO FORM, BAL-ANCING ANXIETY AND NONCHALANCE IN EX-ACTING PROPORTIONS. For some, the approaching storm meant a weekend of preparation. There were windows to board up, kitchens to stock with bottled water and edibles that wouldn't require cooking. Others mastered their fears with prayer or displays of indifference appropriate to The City That Care Forgot: a Saturday night picnic on the Orleans Avenue neutral ground; tickets to the Saints as they played what no one knew would be their last game at the Superdome for a long time to come. Vanna White and Pat Sajak taped a "Wheel of Fortune" installment at the Ernest N. Morial Convention Center, then repaired to Brennan's for a Friday night supper. There was still reason to hope New Orleans' luck would hold. Late Friday, National Weather Service projections of Katrina's likely track jogged east, suggesting a landfall closer to the Alabama-Mississippi line. By Saturday morning, all illusion had been lost. New Orleans was back in the crosshairs.

"LADIES AND GENTLEMEN, THIS IS NOT

As traffic streams out of the city (or tries to), Gina Sannoh, 12, **TOP**, bustles a case of water into the Superdome on Sunday, less than a day before Katrina's strike. With his pooch Princess in his arms, hotel employee Robert LeBlanc, **TOP CENTER**, moves into the Park Plaza on Canal Street to help with guests arriving Sunday to ride out the storm. More typically, tourists, like those on Canal Street, **BOTTOM CENTER**, bail out of their hotels and try to flag down cabs for the airport. Mid-City resident Dan Fuller, **CENTER RIGHT**, strides down Canal Street in search of shelter after trying unsuccessfully to hitchhike out of town. He would shortly catch a bus to the Superdome. By early evening, the interstates and expressways are empty, **FAR RIGHT**.

GETTING OUT

BY LATE SATURDAY AFTERNOON, STATE POLICE HAD MADE ALL LANES ON IN-TERSTATE 10 OUTBOUND FROM NEW ORLEANS to expedite evacuation, and this time — after a disastrously unsuccessful debut a year earlier during Hurricane Ivan — they were determined that the "contraflow" plan would work smoothly.

A TEST. THIS IS THE REAL DEAL." *Mayor Ray Nagin, Saturday, Aug. 27*

The following morning, under pressure from Gov. Kathleen Blanco and Max Mayfield, director of the National Hurricane Center, New Orleans Mayor Ray Nagin made the evacuation mandatory. It would be called the largest and most successful evacuation ever. More than 1 million people escaped southeast Louisiana, some fleeing west toward Texas, others north into Mississippi and Arkansas, a smaller portion rushing to the east, despite concerns that Katrina might chase after them. Some downtown hotels shut down; others welcomed an influx of vertical evacuees, a strategy that would prove regrettable. The largest proportion of those who elected to ride out the storm in New Orleans headed for the Superdome, which would become a scene of unrelieved misery in the days ahead.

The state contraflow plan kicked in Saturday afternoon as cars were funneled across the median strip to make all lanes of Interstate 10 outbound. The Clearview Parkway crossover is visible from different angles in the two pictures at right. But bottlenecks persisted into Sunday afternoon. The motorists, **ABOVE**, were stuck on an I-10 overpass in Kenner.

Pets proved to be a hindrance to the evacuation process. Many residents chose to stay in harm's way rather than abandon cherished cats and dogs. Dweezil was less certain than her owner, Jackie Peterson, that a ride out of town was a good idea.

Residents
flocked to the
Superdome,
but pets were
forbidden.

21

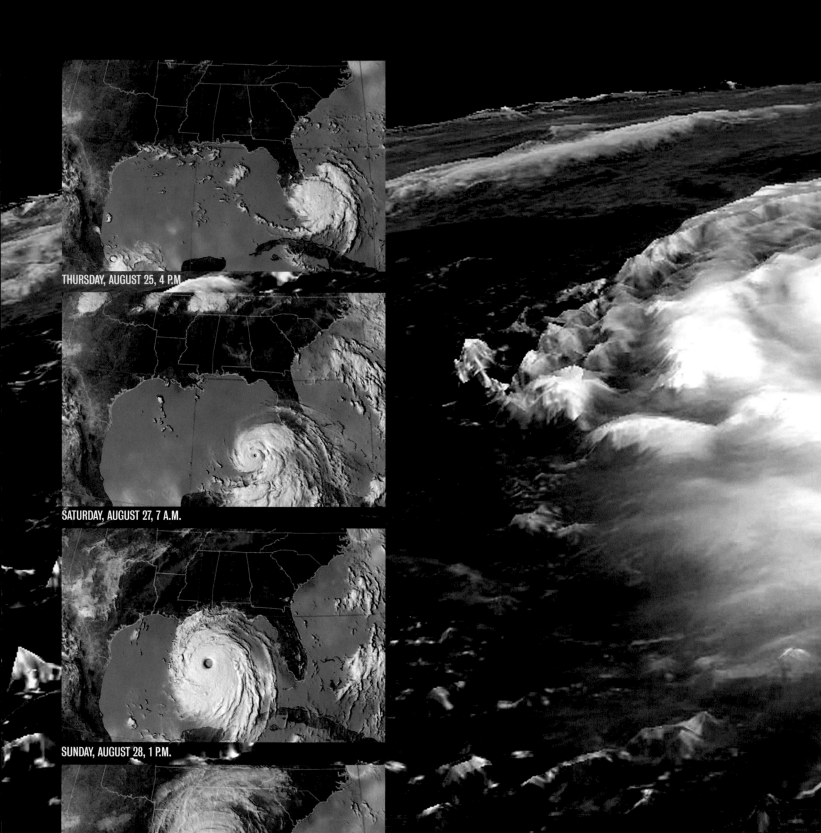

THURSDAY, AUGUST 25, 4 P.M.

SATURDAY, AUGUST 27, 7 A.M.

SUNDAY, AUGUST 28, 1 P.M.

MONDAY, AUGUST 29, 8 A.M.

THE STORM

The Times-Picayune

GROUND ZERO

SUPERDOME BECOMES LAST RESORT FOR THOUSANDS UNABLE TO LEAVE

NEW ORLEANS BRACES FOR NIGHTMARE OF THE BIG ONE

At least 10,000 find refuge at the Superdome

AUG. 29, 2005

THE APPALLING THING ABOUT THE HURRICANE THAT DESTROYED NEW ORLEANS is that by the time Katrina made landfall south of the city, it wasn't the monster it had been — barely a Category 3 event on the five-level Saffir-Simpson scale. But in the Gulf it had been an off-the-chart cyclone, with winds above 155 mph. Its upwelling storm surge was still monstrous by the time it rolled across vanishing wetlands and funneled into local canals and lakes with a force that washed away the federal levee system and drowned 80 percent of the city. At any level of intensity, the sheer size of the storm was one for the record books. The fleecy disk photographed so memorably by satellite was 450 miles across by the time it slammed into the Gulf Coast, laying down a swath of destruction that stretched from Morgan City to Apalachicola Bay, off the Florida Panhandle. In total, 90,000 square miles would be ravaged, an area larger than Great Britain. A diagnostic clue to Katrina's ferocity lies in the thermal imagery at far left, hot water being a hurricane system's sustaining addiction. The orange and red shading indicate water temperatures 82 degrees or higher — hot spots on an increasingly blistered planet that supercharged the storm as it swelled and came ashore.

Katrina's winds whipped city and suburb alike. The rare photo, **ABOVE**, shows the wall of water as it overtopped levees under the Paris Road bridge in eastern New Orleans just west of the Mississippi River–Gulf Outlet, a waterway implicated in having worsened the storm surge by channeling it deep into the heart of the city.

Lt. Darren Minvielle watches storm waters claim Kenner's Williams Boulevard as Katrina passes over. **LEFT**, newly planted palms are toppled and banners shredded as the hurricane lashes Canal Street in New Orleans on Monday morning. But much greater menace lay in the storm surge that rolled in from the Gulf.

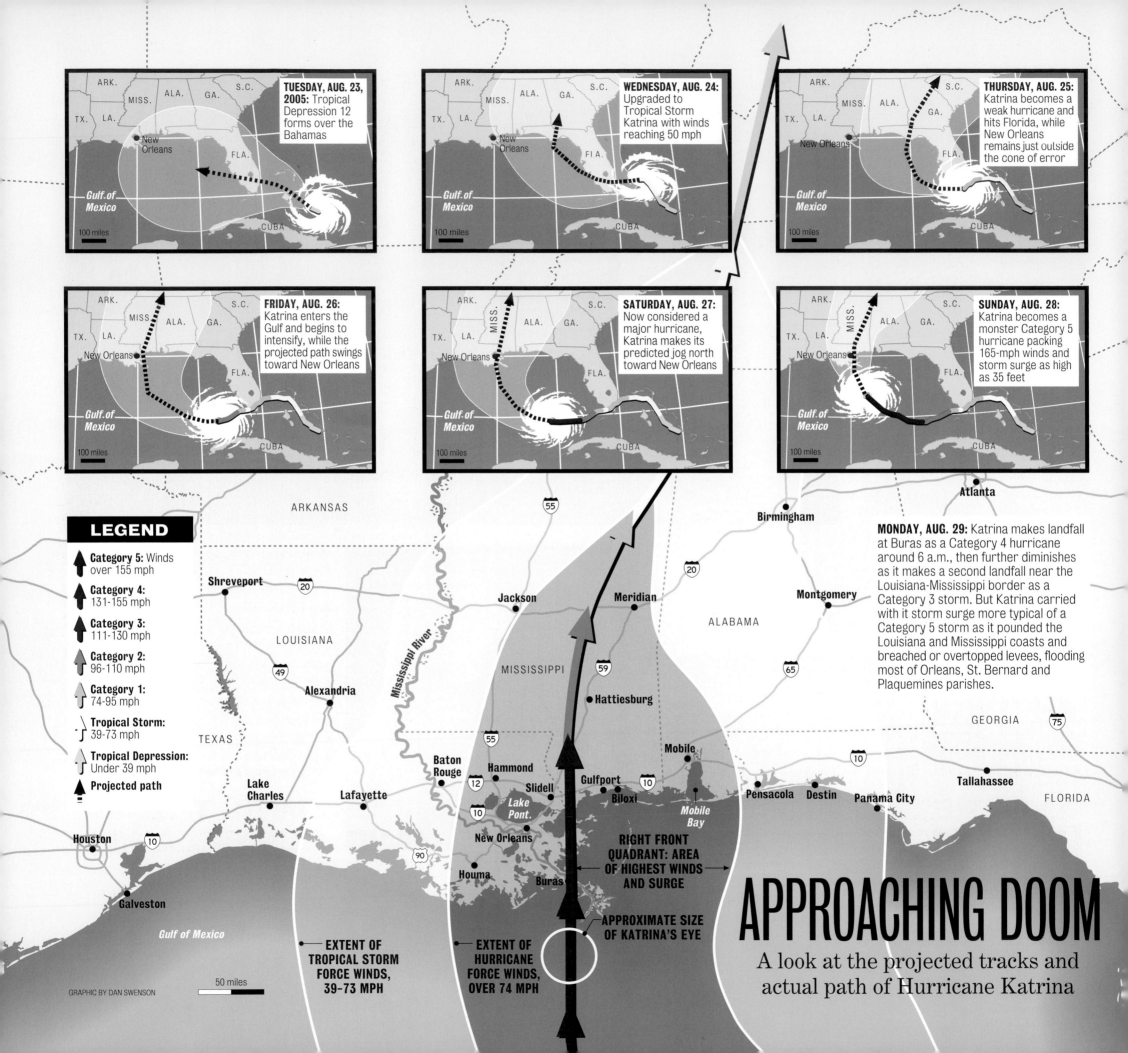

TUESDAY, AUG. 23, 2005: Tropical Depression 12 forms over the Bahamas

WEDNESDAY, AUG. 24: Upgraded to Tropical Storm Katrina with winds reaching 50 mph

THURSDAY, AUG. 25: Katrina becomes a weak hurricane and hits Florida, while New Orleans remains just outside the cone of error

FRIDAY, AUG. 26: Katrina enters the Gulf and begins to intensify, while the projected path swings toward New Orleans

SATURDAY, AUG. 27: Now considered a major hurricane, Katrina makes its predicted jog north toward New Orleans

SUNDAY, AUG. 28: Katrina becomes a monster Category 5 hurricane packing 165-mph winds and storm surge as high as 35 feet

MONDAY, AUG. 29: Katrina makes landfall at Buras as a Category 4 hurricane around 6 a.m., then further diminishes as it makes a second landfall near the Louisiana-Mississippi border as a Category 3 storm. But Katrina carried with it storm surge more typical of a Category 5 storm as it pounded the Louisiana and Mississippi coasts and breached or overtopped levees, flooding most of Orleans, St. Bernard and Plaquemines parishes.

LEGEND

Category 5: Winds over 155 mph
Category 4: 131-155 mph
Category 3: 111-130 mph
Category 2: 96-110 mph
Category 1: 74-95 mph
Tropical Storm: 39-73 mph
Tropical Depression: Under 39 mph
Projected path

RIGHT FRONT QUADRANT: AREA OF HIGHEST WINDS AND SURGE

APPROXIMATE SIZE OF KATRINA'S EYE

EXTENT OF TROPICAL STORM FORCE WINDS, 39-73 MPH

EXTENT OF HURRICANE FORCE WINDS, OVER 74 MPH

APPROACHING DOOM
A look at the projected tracks and actual path of Hurricane Katrina

GRAPHIC BY DAN SWENSON

50 miles

Telephone poles as well as trees were casualties of the storm as it pushed Lake Pontchartrain into western St. Tammany Parish, including a stretch of Louisiana 22, near the fashionable Beau Chene residential subdivision.

"PINE TREES BOW TO THE FEROCIOUS WINDS UNTIL THE TREES SNAP LIKE TWIGS IN A CHILD'S HAND. ONE BREAKS SEVERAL FEET FROM ITS BASE, THEN ANOTHER, THEN DOZENS, LIKE POPCORN BEGINNING TO POP ON A KITCHEN STOVE. ...WE WAIT FOR THE TREE THAT WILL SMASH THE HOUSE — AND US."

Times-Picayune reporter Leslie Williams, who rode out the storm with his family on the Mississippi Gulf Coast

THE SCOPE OF THE DESTRUCTION WAS AS ASTONISHING AS ITS VARIETY. Each hour Katrina unleashed energy equivalent in its fury to five atomic bombs of the size dropped on Hiroshima, scientists estimated. At left, a community of homes — including two U-Haul trucks — was reduced to flotsam on the shores of Lake Pontchartrain at Slidell. The storm sucked a wall of win- dows out of the Hyatt Regency Hotel, where Mayor Ray Nagin and much of city government sought refuge on the 27th floor after abandon- ing the emergency operations center in City Hall. Yachts and smaller sailboats were strewn about a New Orleans marina like toy boats in a bathtub. Attesting to the ecological havoc wrought by the storm, min-

MICHAEL DeMOCKER

nows lay dead in a St. Bernard Parish street. The more ominous loss was to coastal wetlands where the fish breed. In hours, Katrina erased more than 100 square miles of Louisiana's coastal marsh, or more than ordinarily is lost in a year, further reducing the buffer that lies between a rampant storm surge and the population centers of southeast Louisiana.

STORM TOLL

CHRIS GRANGER

JOHN McCUSKER

Little more than pilings remain along Slidell's Rat's Nest Road, **ABOVE**, once a teeming aquatic village of fishing camps and larger structures built out over Lake Pontchartrain. The apartment complex in eastern New Orleans, **RIGHT**, didn't fare much better. Indeed, the devastation in the east took a particularly heavy toll on the city's low- to medium-priced rental market.

DAVID GRUNFELD

TED JACKSON

MICHAEL DeMOCKER

MICHAEL DeMOCKER

Along Elysian Fields Avenue in New Orleans' Gentilly district, Bishop Darryl S. Brister's wife, Dionne Flot Brister, smiles winsomely from a shattered billboard for Beacon Light International Baptist Cathedral.

At first glance, damage to this church might seem limited to the shingles lost to Katrina's winds. On closer inspection, it's possible to see the concrete steps and footings where the building stood before storm surge lifted it off its foundation and carried it dozens of yards from its former site, in Empire, a fishing village in Plaquemines Parish about 50 miles downriver from New Orleans.

ABOVE, pilings mark the site of a cluster of seafood restaurants — Bruning's and Jaeger's among them — that were a mecca for generations of New Orleanians, drawn to the city's West End and the Lake Pontchartrain waterfront.

RIGHT, storm surge flowing into Lake Pontchartrain devastates the Interstate 10 twin spans connecting eastern New Orleans with St. Tammany Parish and the Mississippi coast.

FAR RIGHT, giant trawlers used for harvesting menhaden are strewn across Louisiana 23 at Empire, the Plaquemines Parish fishing village all but completely wiped out by Katrina.

A single hoist and its cover are all that remain of Blackie Campo's marina at Shell Beach on Lake Borgne, a popular boat launch for New Orleans anglers.

BCB MARSHALL

SCOTT THRELKELD

athy Wood had spent one day in the townhouse she renovated on Lakeview Drive near Slidell before Katrina ...stroyed the place. The refrigerator, which had been on the second floor, turns up a quarter-mile away, with ...mily snapshots still taped to the door.

By Wednesday, Susan Lassiter had returned to her Finley Street home in Gulfport, Miss., with her husband, Ford, to search for anything salvageable and to ward off looters.

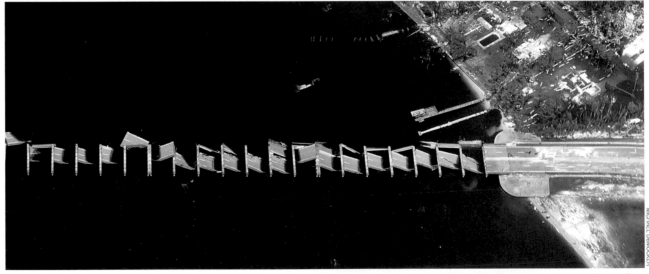

The bridge from Bay St. Louis to Pass Christian in Mississippi is another casualty of Katrina. Gulfport, **RIGHT**, a day after Katrina made landfall, typifies the devastation that extended from Waveland all the way to Pascagoula, hammering Bay St. Louis, Pass Christian and Biloxi on the way.

The Mississippi Gulf Coast's experience of Katrina was not a matter of destruction, but of utter eradication. A monster wall of water more than 30 feet high in some places surged up from the sea, turning shoreline roads into beaches and block after block of houses into flotsam.

As the hurricane begins to intensify, flying gravel shatters most of the windows in his van, parked behind the Holiday Inn, and Jimmy Lowe Jr. of Bay St. Louis, Miss., rushes to retrieve items from the vehicle.

The dolphins, **ABOVE**, were not flung from the Gulf into the Holiday Inn swimming pool on Route 49. They were placed there by Gulfport's Marine Life Oceanarium, after testing the water to make sure the chemical balance made it a safe place for them to ride out the storm.

A young woman in St. Bernard Parish attempts a swim to safety along flooded St. Claude Avenue, close to the Orleans Parish line.

THE GREAT INUNDATION

AUG. 30, 2005

NEW ORLEANS HAD DODGED THE BULLET. That was the impression in some parts of town — and in the upper echelons of the Bush administration — as Katrina's cyclonic winds began to subside Monday afternoon. It was a grievous misdiagnosis. Even before Katrina reached the city, some neighborhoods were under water — those lying to the east. Storm surge had knocked down levees along the coast and toppled the concrete flood-walls of the Industrial Canal after barreling up the Mississippi River-Gulf Outlet and into the Intracoastal Canal. The surge had turned those shipping channels into water cannons aimed at the heart of the city. Almost at once, Lower 9th Ward houses were knocked off their footings and drifted into the streets. Then, late Monday, water began to rise mysteriously in downtown streets, slipping through doors and around the windows of buildings that had never been submerged. Breaches in the 17th Street and London Avenue canals had widened catastrophically, and Lake Pontchartrain was sweeping into the city: the long-dreaded "worst-case scenario" for a city below sea level. It would be Thursday — 40 billion gallons later — before the water levels within and outside the levees had been equalized. Eighty percent of New Orleans was under water.

On Thursday, three days after Katrina made landfall, the view toward downtown New Orleans from Airline Drive in suburban Jefferson Parish is of Atlantis, a city submerged.

Interstate 610 at the St. Bernard Avenue exit plunges into the brackish swill that has engulfed the city's Gentilly neighborhood, providing a handy ramp for launching rescue boats.

"I WAS TALKING TO MY MOTHER ON THE PHONE AT 8 IN THE MORNING, TELLING HER EVERYTHING WAS FINE. THEN, NEXT THING YOU KNOW, IT'S JUST GUSHING, GUSHING, GUSHING, AND WE CAN'T OPEN THE DOOR, AND THEN THE WATER WAS UP TO MY NECK."

Joan Hanson, who swam from her home in St. Bernard to the roof of a relative's home where she and her son were later rescued

Like leaves in a storm drain, uprooted houses swirl aimlessly in the streets of the Lower 9th Ward after the district is inundated by the breached Industrial Canal that forms its western boundary.

Floodwaters burst the doors of aboveground crypts and rip the lids from surface-level graves.

At Buras, where Katrina made her Louisiana landfall, the town's water tower is a casualty of the winds and rampant surge.

Waters engulf an interstate cloverleaf near the Orleans-Jefferson parish line and swamp the pumping station, above, that had been recently added to the city's flood-control infrastructure. The pumping station was designed to prevent repeated inundation of the dip below a railroad overpass in the distance beyond it.

TOP LEFT, a resident of the Lower 9th Ward squeezes through an attic window and onto the roof of his house before flagging down a rescue boat. Farther down St. Claude Avenue that same Monday afternoon, two young women huddle above floodwaters still rising across the Lower 9th Ward. In eastern New Orleans, **BELOW**, a man peers anxiously from his house, engulfed in Katrina's lethal surge.

TED JACKSON

CLOCKWISE FROM TOP LEFT, Roosevelt Kyles holds a sack of diabetes medicines in his mouth as he emerges from his 9th Ward home and prepares to board a rescue boat. A FEMA rescue worker hacks a hole in a Lakeview roof, too late to save the elderly man trapped inside. Their house adrift, two men await rescue on a roof in St. Bernard Parish.

A rescued Lois Rice musters a faint smile as she is carried by boat from the Lower 9th Ward.

ALEX BRANDON

ALEX BRANDON

With their valuables in plastic sacks, a Mid-City couple floats their dog on a makeshift raft as they wade across Canal Street, two days after Katrina.

Farther along Canal Street, in the city's downtown area, knots of survivors flock toward dry ground along the riverfront, some 10 blocks ahead.

44

A New Orleans Police Department SWAT team ferries women and children to the St. Claude Avenue bridge that connects the devastated Lower 9th Ward to the less heavily flooded area west of the Industrial Canal.

TED JACKSON

The hurricane has passed and the flooding has begun Monday afternoon as three men — John Rainey, John Rainey Jr. and Courtney Davis — help Terry Fox tug a tub full of children toward an overpass on South Broad Street.

45

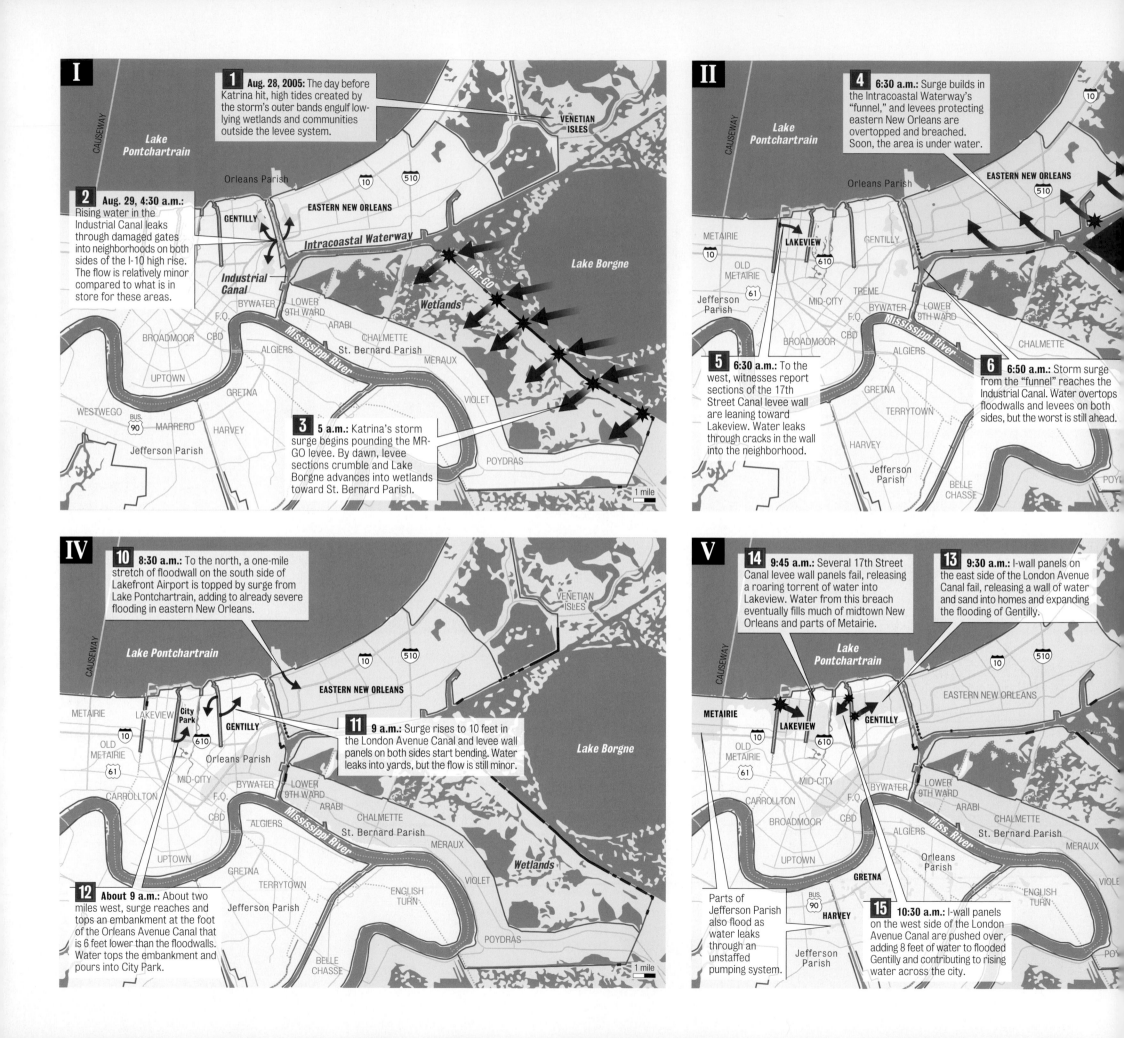

I

1 **Aug. 28, 2005:** The day before Katrina hit, high tides created by the storm's outer bands engulf low-lying wetlands and communities outside the levee system.

2 **Aug. 29, 4:30 a.m.:** Rising water in the Industrial Canal leaks through damaged gates into neighborhoods on both sides of the I-10 high rise. The flow is relatively minor compared to what is in store for these areas.

3 **5 a.m.:** Katrina's storm surge begins pounding the MR-GO levee. By dawn, levee sections crumble and Lake Borgne advances into wetlands toward St. Bernard Parish.

II

4 **6:30 a.m.:** Surge builds in the Intracoastal Waterway's "funnel," and levees protecting eastern New Orleans are overtopped and breached. Soon, the area is under water.

5 **6:30 a.m.:** To the west, witnesses report sections of the 17th Street Canal levee wall are leaning toward Lakeview. Water leaks through cracks in the wall into the neighborhood.

6 **6:50 a.m.:** Storm surge from the "funnel" reaches the Industrial Canal. Water overtops floodwalls and levees on both sides, but the worst is still ahead.

IV

10 **8:30 a.m.:** To the north, a one-mile stretch of floodwall on the south side of Lakefront Airport is topped by surge from Lake Pontchartrain, adding to already severe flooding in eastern New Orleans.

11 **9 a.m.:** Surge rises to 10 feet in the London Avenue Canal and levee wall panels on both sides start bending. Water leaks into yards, but the flow is still minor.

12 **About 9 a.m.:** About two miles west, surge reaches and tops an embankment at the foot of the Orleans Avenue Canal that is 6 feet lower than the floodwalls. Water tops the embankment and pours into City Park.

V

14 **9:45 a.m.:** Several 17th Street Canal levee wall panels fail, releasing a roaring torrent of water into Lakeview. Water from this breach eventually fills much of midtown New Orleans and parts of Metairie.

13 **9:30 a.m.:** I-wall panels on the east side of the London Avenue Canal fail, releasing a wall of water and sand into homes and expanding the flooding of Gentilly.

Parts of Jefferson Parish also flood as water leaks through an unstaffed pumping system.

15 **10:30 a.m.:** I-wall panels on the west side of the London Avenue Canal are pushed over, adding 8 feet of water to flooded Gentilly and contributing to rising water across the city.

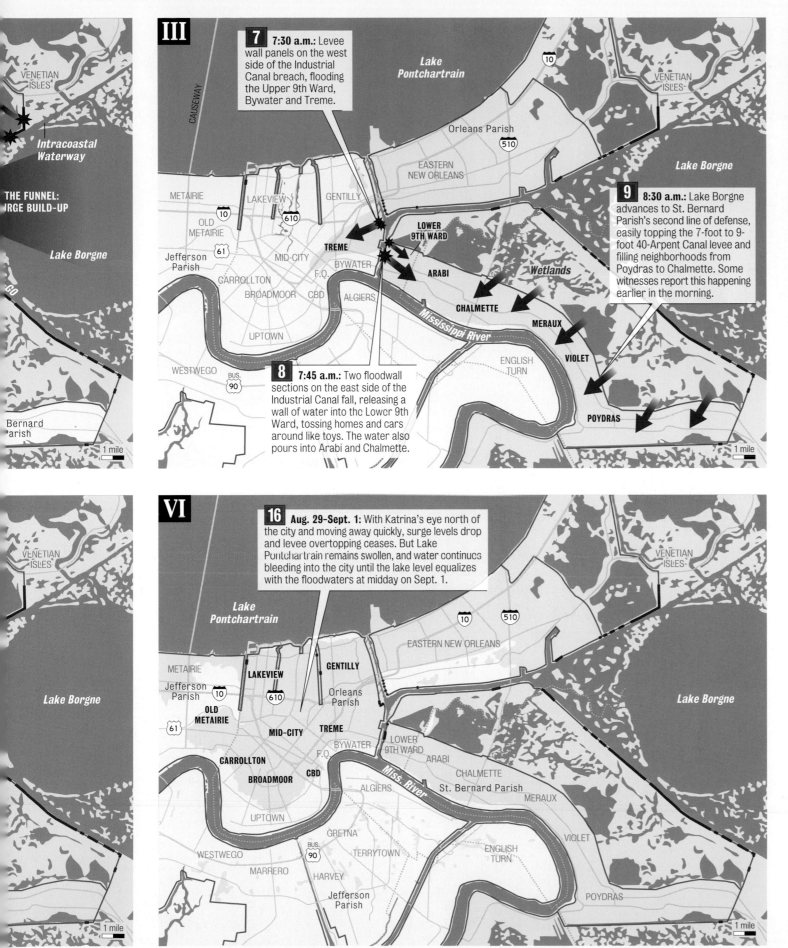

III

7 **7:30 a.m.:** Levee wall panels on the west side of the Industrial Canal breach, flooding the Upper 9th Ward, Bywater and Treme.

8 **7:45 a.m.:** Two floodwall sections on the east side of the Industrial Canal fall, releasing a wall of water into the Lower 9th Ward, tossing homes and cars around like toys. The water also pours into Arabi and Chalmette.

9 **8:30 a.m.:** Lake Borgne advances to St. Bernard Parish's second line of defense, easily topping the 7-foot to 9-foot 40-Arpent Canal levee and filling neighborhoods from Poydras to Chalmette. Some witnesses report this happening earlier in the morning.

THE FUNNEL: JRGE BUILD-UP

VENETIAN ISLES

Intracoastal Waterway

Lake Borgne

Bernard Parish

METAIRIE
OLD METAIRIE
Jefferson Parish
MID-CITY
GARROLLTON
BROADMOOR
CBD
UPTOWN
WESTWEGO
LAKEVIEW
TREME
BYWATER
F.Q.
ALGIERS
GENTILLY
LOWER 9TH WARD
ARABI
CHALMETTE
MERAUX
VIOLET
POYDRAS
ENGLISH TURN

Lake Pontchartrain
Orleans Parish
EASTERN NEW ORLEANS
Wetlands
Mississippi River

VENETIAN ISLES
Lake Borgne

CAUSEWAY

1 mile

VI

16 **Aug. 29-Sept. 1:** With Katrina's eye north of the city and moving away quickly, surge levels drop and levee overtopping ceases. But Lake Pontchartrain remains swollen, and water continues bleeding into the city until the lake level equalizes with the floodwaters at midday on Sept. 1.

VENETIAN ISLES

Lake Borgne

METAIRIE
Jefferson Parish
OLD METAIRIE
MID-CITY
GARROLLTON
BROADMOOR
CBD
UPTOWN
WESTWEGO
MARRERO
HARVEY
Jefferson Parish
LAKEVIEW
TREME
BYWATER
F.Q.
ALGIERS
GRETNA
TERRYTOWN
GENTILLY
Orleans Parish
LOWER 9TH WARD
ARABI
CHALMETTE
St. Bernard Parish
MERAUX
VIOLET
ENGLISH TURN
POYDRAS

Lake Pontchartrain
EASTERN NEW ORLEANS

VENETIAN ISLES
Lake Borgne

Miss. River

1 mile

1 mile

SWEPT BY A DEADLY SURGE

Beginning with a small leak along the Industrial Canal, a series of escalating calamities unfolded over six hours early on the morning of Monday, Aug. 29, 2005, as Hurricane Katrina passed over the city. By early afternoon, even before key officials knew what had happened, the city was inundated.

LEGEND

⌐ Levees and/or floodwalls
⌐ Compromised levee
✳ Breach
▢ Flooded land
▢ Existing waterways and water bodies
➜ Water flow

GRAPHIC BY DAN SWENSON
Sources: LSU Hurricane Center, Army Corps of Engineers
IPET report, Dartmouth Flood Observatory, witness accounts

On the front lines

Reporting the story of the century

On Monday about noon, photographer Ted Jackson waded down into the flooded Lower 9th Ward. Almost at once he was accosted by the women and children, pictured left. Perched on the porch railing where they had been trapped for hours, they cried out to him for help. It made for an excruciating dilemma.

TED JACKSON
Times-Picayune photographer

"They wanted to know if I was there to help them," Jackson recalls. To an elderly man on the ramp with Jackson, it was deeply offensive that the photographer should be plying his trade in the face of human suffering. "We'll talk about it over lunch someday," Jackson said, firing off a few shots. "This is my job. We need to have a record of what's going on here." Jackson turned back to the women. "The wind was still howling; the rain had slacked up a bit, but we had to yell at each other," Jackson recalls. "They were desperately trying to get the kids across the street. There's a log in the picture and this little girl is balancing on the log and they were trying to get the girl onto the log to push her across. They were trying to get the other little girl into the ice chest to keep her afloat. It was obviously a tragedy waiting to happen. I decided I couldn't just stay there and watch the children drown. I begged them to just keep holding on, that boats would be arriving soon."

> "I DECIDED I COULDN'T JUST STAY THERE AND WATCH THE CHILDREN DROWN. I BEGGED THEM TO JUST KEEP HOLDING ON, THAT BOATS WOULD BE ARRIVING SOON."

Jackson returned to the newspaper's downtown office and borrowed an inflatable Zodiak. But when he got back the porch was ominously empty. The women and children were gone. "There were a couple of boats in the water, a couple of Police Department boats, a SWAT team. The first thing I asked: 'Did you get the family on the porch?' And they said, 'What family? What porch?' I assumed that they had all drowned."

Months later, Jackson found himself in the neighborhood and slipped into the abandoned house. Amid the detritus he found a sheet of paper with a name on it. A reporter traced the family for him. "They had been rescued and were safe in Houston," Jackson learned. He placed a call and one of the women answered. The first words out of her mouth were accusing: "The thing that we couldn't understand was why you left us." Jackson explained himself: "'It's very important to me for you to know that I came back with a boat.' And she said, 'I didn't know that.' The last thing she said was, 'Can you send us a copy of the picture? I want to see the picture.'"

DEPTH OF DISASTER

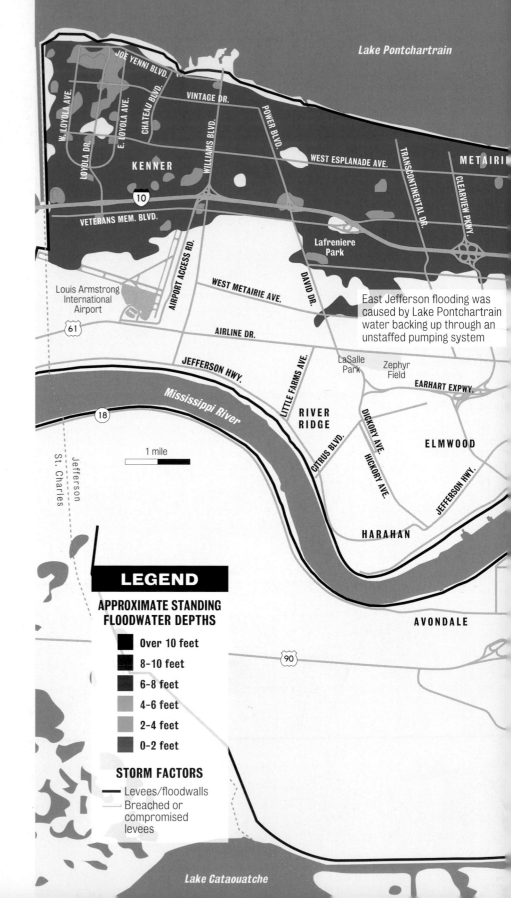

East Jefferson flooding was caused by Lake Pontchartrain water backing up through an unstaffed pumping system

LEGEND

APPROXIMATE STANDING FLOODWATER DEPTHS

- Over 10 feet
- 8-10 feet
- 6-8 feet
- 4-6 feet
- 2-4 feet
- 0-2 feet

STORM FACTORS

- Levees/floodwalls
- Breached or compromised levees

Levee breaches from Katrina's monster surge left the city under more than 10 feet of floodwater in some neighborhoods. A look at the maximum standing water depths at the height of the flood, when Lake Pontchartrain leveled off with New Orleans:

17th Street Canal

Orleans Avenue Canal

London Avenue Canal

Industrial Canal

Lakefront Airport

SEVERN AVE.

CAUSEWAY BLVD.

BUCKTOWN

LAKEVIEW

UNO

GENTILLY

FRANKLIN

PRESS DR.

LEON C. SIMON DR.

ROBERT E. LEE BLVD.

WEST END BLVD.

GARRISON

City Park

GENTILLY BLVD.

ELYSIAN FIELDS AVE.

HAYNE BLVD.

DOWMAN RD.

LAKE FOREST BLVD.

MICHOUD BLVD.

VILLAGE DE L'EST

10

510

90

CHEF MENTEUR HWY.

ALMONASTER AVE.

Intracoastal Waterway

Miss. River-Gulf Outlet

BONNABEL BLVD.

VETERANS BLVD.

10

WEST NAPOLEON AVE.

METAIRIE ROAD

OLD METAIRIE

CITY PARK AVE.

ST. BERNARD AVE.

ORLEANS

BROAD

ESPLANADE

NEW ORLEANS

FLORIDA

Orleans
St. Bernard

Wetlands

PARIS ROAD

AIRLINE DR.

61

MID-CITY

PALMETTO

CARROLLTON AVE.

TULANE

TREME

10

ST. CLAUDE

BYWATER

TUPELO

LOWER 9TH WARD

ARABI

PATRICIA

JEAN LAFITTE PKWY.

JUDGE PEREZ DR.

ROWLEY BLVD.

CHALMETTE

39

FERSON EIGHTS

RD.

FARHART BLVD.

CLAIBORNE AVE.

WASHINGTON

10

CARROLLTON

BACK...

FRENCH QUARTER

CANAL

Superdome

CBD

NEWTON

ALGIERS

GEN. MEYER AVE.

Mississippi River

46

47

ST. BERNARD HWY.

GOLDEN DR.

PALMIS...

MUNS...

ARCHBISHOP HANNAN BLVD.

MERAUX

BROADWAY

NASHVILLE

ST. CHARLES AVE.

NAPOLEON AVE.

UPTOWN

LOUISIANA AVE.

GARDEN DISTRICT

GEN. DE GAULLE DR.

MAC ARTHUR BLVD.

WOODLAND DR.

Orleans
Jefferson

LEGEND DR.

MERAUX LN.

39

18

Audubon Park

MAGAZINE

TCHOUPITOULAS

GRETNA

HOLMES BLVD.

406

ENGLISH TURN

Orleans
Plaquemines

LOUISIANA

4TH

LAFAYETTE

WEST BANK EXPWY.

TERRYTOWN

TERRY PKWY.

BEHRMAN HWY.

46

WEST BANK EXPWY.

MARRERO

PETERS RD.

BUS. 90

HARVEY

GRETNA BLVD.

MANHATTAN BLVD.

BELLE CHASSE HWY.

WESTWEGO

Some parts of the West Bank also flooded due to an unstaffed pumping system

BARATARIA BLVD.

Harvey Canal

23

LAPALCO BLVD.

AMES BLVD.

45

BELLE CHASSE

39

GRAPHIC BY DAN SWENSON
Source: C&C Technologies
Survey Services

HELLISH SHELTERS

KATRINA: THE STORM WE'VE ALWAYS FEARED

The Times-Picayune

'HELP US, PLEASE'

AFTER THE DISASTER, CHAOS AND
LAWLESSNESS RULE THE STREETS

Local leaders call relief
efforts too little, too late

Blanco
demands
thousands
of troops

SEPT. 2, 2005

AN INFANT IN HIS ARMS, A CORPSE SLUMPED IN THE LAWN CHAIR AT HIS SIDE, a refugee endures the chaos and gross privation that was the Ernest N. Morial Convention Center in the week after Katrina struck the city. Even before the hurricane made landfall, throngs had flocked to the Superdome, the city's unofficial shelter of last resort. Lashing winds ripped open the roof, the electricity failed and within hours of the storm's passage, the Dome's 20,000 occupants were stewing in a brew of fetid air; backed-up sewage and mounting tension that would claim at least six lives, one of them a suicide who hurled himself from a stadium balcony. Now came an added influx of refugees, as boats and helicopters began plucking survivors off rooftops and elevated roadways. By Tuesday, the Dome had absorbed another 5,000 helpless people and the overflow — an additional 20,000 — was being shunted a dozen blocks down Poydras Street to the riverfront Convention Center. If the Dome had been ill-equipped, the Convention Center was utterly without provisions for the small and increasingly desperate city that was soon encamped there.

TED JACKSON

"WE'RE HURTING OUT HERE, MAN. WE GOT TO GET HELP. ALL

Tasheka Johnson, 24, who was among thousands who were trapped for days at the Ernest N. Morial Convention Center

Glum, resigned and yet orderly and patient, storm survivors stranded at the Ernest N. Morial Convention Center line the curb three days after the storm, as rumors spread that an armada of buses was at last approaching the city to whisk them to safety. In fact, it would be another two days before the last people would be transported from the sprawling and ill-managed shelter.

Katrina spared neither the young nor the ancient, nor people of any age in between. Elmore Gibson, 83, is helped out of a boat that carried him through floodwaters to the Superdome.

Still awaiting rescue four days after Katrina struck, 1-year-old Nicholas Herbert takes a slug of water from his mama's bottle as they cross a Convention Center parking lot.

VE WANT IS SOMEONE TO FEEL OUR PAIN, THAT'S ALL."

There was nothing private about life in the shelters, not for the living, not for the dead. But at the very center of the Superdome's artificial turf, Clifford Coates, 23, catches at least a few winks in relative isolation within the 50-yard-line fleur-de-lis that is the emblem of New Orleans and its NFL team, the Saints.

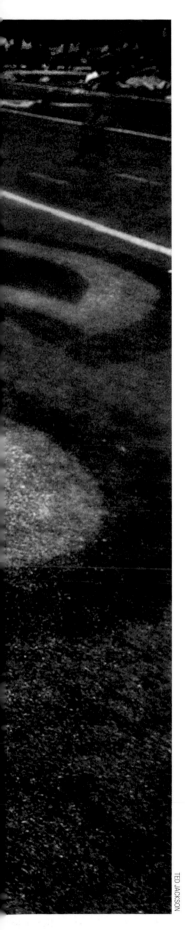

As the week grinds on, the unbearable stench and clamor within the Convention Center drive refugees out onto the sidewalks, **ABOVE LEFT.** But others remain inside, **TOP RIGHT,** too exhausted to do anything more than sit or doze. For Ethel Freeman, 91, the sleep was eternal. Alongside another anonymous storm victim shrouded in a bedsheet, Freeman's wheelchair-bound corpse sits in front of the Convention Center four days after the storm, a symbol of neglect and the failure of a relief effort that by then had become inarguably a fiasco.

For Anita Roach, **BELOW,** the misery of the Convention Center is eased by leading those around her in gospel songs of praise and supplication, five days after the storm had passed. For Carla Weisshahn, a Wisconsonite who was vacationing in New Orleans when Katrina trapped her among fellow refugees, the horrors and sheer boredom of her week in hell were relieved by acts of service to others. Here she helps New Orleanian Velma Brosa, **RIGHT,** to a bite of military rations.

ALEX BRANDON

CHRIS GRANGER

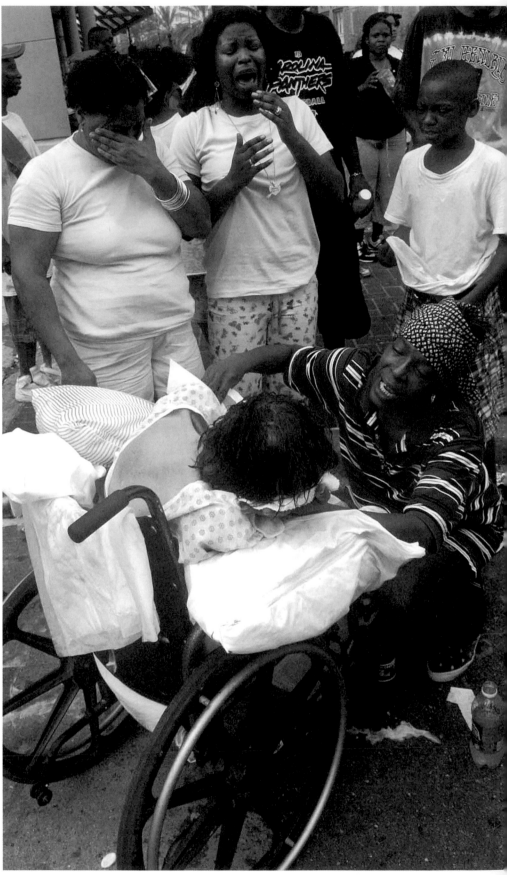

Health worker Terri Johnson, in bandanna, **RIGHT,** begs and cajoles her charge, 89-year-old Dorothy "Miss Dot" Duvic, not to give up as dehydration and heatstroke brought Duvic near death on Thursday outside the Convention Center. In hopes of finding a West Bank hospital for Duvic, Johnson later pushed her up onto the Crescent City Connection bridge, only to be stopped by armed men. A passer-by agreed to carry them to West Jefferson Medical Center in his pickup. Duvic was transferred to nursing homes in Lafayette and then Monroe, where she died on Jan. 8. Her Gentilly home destroyed by flooding, Johnson moved to Houston and began rebuilding her life.

n the roadway along the front of the Convention Center, Angela Perkins acts out the despair that swept a city as help failed to arrive.

By week's end, soldiers and buses begin to arrive in force. Lines of refugees snake through the Warehouse District within blocks of the Convention Center, all awaiting their turn to embark for — Baton Rouge? Texas? Arkansas? Many passengers were not told where they were headed until after their journey was well under way.

CHRIS GRANGER

On the front lines

Reporting the story of the century

TRYMAINE LEE

Times-Picayune reporter

I had seen a city drown, then take what seemed to be its last breath. But somehow the full impact of Katrina still hadn't hit me. It took a woman named Lucrece to make me grasp the horror that was unfolding.

People were crowded into every crevice of the dark, dank lobby of the Hyatt Regency Hotel, where I had come with another reporter and officials forced out of City Hall when the basement flooded. The stench of our unbathed bodies wafted on the already heavy air.

In the darkness I heard a woman crying. It was Lucrece Phillips, who hours earlier had been rescued from the Lower 9th Ward with six of her family members. Rescuers had dumped her at the Superdome, where soldiers "treated us like animals," she later told me. Phillips was hugging a big, burly rescue worker, fistfuls of his sweaty blue T-shirt rippling in her hands as she cried on his chest. She backed away, still crying, mouthing a few more thank-yous. I walked up and put an arm around her. Tears streaked her cheeks and rolled down my forearm as she told me her story.

"The rescuers in the boats that picked us up had to push the bodies back with sticks," she sobbed. "And there was this little baby. She looked so perfect and so beautiful. I just wanted to scoop her up and breathe life back into her little lungs. She wasn't bloated or anything, just perfect." In that moment I began to fathom the magnitude of the catastrophe. A woman I'd encountered earlier in the day, trudging down Poydras Street with her belongings in a bag and a baby on her hip, was just a small piece of it. The young man I met leaving the Dome that afternoon – who said he'd rather die on the streets than endure another minute in the fetid shelter – was another.

"LUCRECE'S DISMAY WAS CONTAGIOUS, AND SOON I WAS CRYING WITH HER, WHILE TRYING TO WRITE DOWN WHAT SHE WAS TELLING ME ABOUT HER DOWNSTAIRS NEIGHBORS, A MOTHER AND A 5-YEAR-OLD SON WHO HAD PERISHED IN THE FLOOD."

Lucrece's dismay was contagious, and soon I was crying with her, while trying to write down what she was telling me about her downstairs neighbors, a mother and a 5-year-old son who had perished in the flood. "I can still hear them banging on the ceiling for help," Lucrece said, shaking. "I heard them banging and banging, but the water kept rising." Intuition told her — correctly — that the death toll would be staggering: "All those people, all them black people, drowned." Lucrece's account figured centrally in my coverage that day. She was able to put into words the trauma that so many thousands of people survived — or died trying to survive.

A week after Katrina, a New Orleans police SWAT team, **FAR RIGHT,** descends a motionless escalator in the Convention Center in a search for any holdouts still lurking in the giant building. **RIGHT,** by the following Friday, a crew in anti-contamination suits has begun cleaning the Superdome of its squalor and filth.

As the Convention Center is evacuated, National Guardsmen tend to a woman who has collapsed while waiting for help.

Debris from within the Convention Center is pushed out to the curb for eventual pickup.

SACKING THE CITY

PEOPLE WATCHING FROM ALL ACROSS THE COUNTRY SAW THE LOOTING TWO WAYS: AS THE MEASURE OF AN ABANDONED CITY'S DESPERATION — AND ALSO OF ITS DEPRAVITY. Whether motivated by urgent need or sheer greed, the pillaging was epic in scale and not at all helpful at a time when New Orleans had turned to the nation, begging for an outpouring of sympathy and support. But much of it could be forgiven, only more so as the week dragged on without the federal government figuring out how to mount an effective relief effort. Mothers with babies in their arms  grabbed bottles of milk and bags of bread, not without helping themselves to a six-pack of beer. Young men hotwired cars, loaded them with friends and neighbors and got out of Dodge. Under city disaster plans, police and certain other public employees were authorized to commandeer what they needed in an emergency. But civil order disintegrated, and a startling number of cops seemed to lose their heads to an orgy of thievery in which they took everything from jewelry to high-priced automobiles. At left, the Cajun Market on Convention Center Boulevard is stripped bare by looters too frenzied to notice that their rampage is being recorded by a photographer. By midweek, Mayor Ray Nagin had ordered officers to abandon rescue efforts and join with soldiers in a campaign to retake a city that had spun out of control.

Police and DEA officers patrolling Elysian Fields Avenue confront two young men who lift their shirts to show they aren't armed. "We live here," the young men tell them. "No one lives here anymore," the officers retort as they move through the city enforcing a mandatory evacuation on the first week's anniversary of Katrina.

New Orleans police officer Fred Fath covers the perimeter as an NOPD SWAT team prepares to search for looters who shot at police in the Central Business District three days after Katrina.

ALEX BRANDON

Some of the most wanton and aggressive looting — by police and civilians alike — is visited upon an Uptown Wal-Mart Supercenter. The vast emporium is picked almost clean, though Harbor Police are able to secure the guns and ammunition in the hunting department before these weapons could fall to marauders.

Hours after the hurricane struck and just before the area would begin filling with water, young men haul bags of merchandise looted from a discount clothing outlet off Earhart Boulevard in New Orleans.

KATI-Y ANDERSON

ALEX BRANDON

New Orleans K-9 cops take down a group of suspected looters near the Convention Center three days after Katrina.

65

His ranks augmented with a variety of federal agents, Capt. Jeff Winn, right, commander of the New Orleans Police Department's SWAT team, prepares his troops to scour the Fischer public housing development for firearms.

A shirtless man seeking a ride away from the mayhem of the Convention Center accosts a police cruiser with a missing rear window.

A New Orleans police officer leaves Wal-Mart with a handful of DVDs. Police offered diverse explanations for how merchandise, including a slew of high-priced automobiles, wound up in officers' hands. Some cops were reinstated; others were fired.

TED JACKSON

ORIENTAL RUGS
ANTIQUE AND NEW

DONT TRY,
I AM SLEEPING
INSIDE WITH
A BIG DOG,
AN UGLY WOMAN,
TWO SHOTGUNS
AND A CLAW HAMMER

LOOTERS
WILL BE
SHOT

9/4/05
STILL HERE
WOMAN
LEFT FRI.
COOKING
A POT OF
DOG
GUMBO

MICHAEL DeMOCKER

The graffiti is lighthearted, the Texas Army National Guardsman less so as he stands sentry in front of a rug shop on St. Charles Avenue 11 days after Katrina.

SUSAN POAG

As the federal relief effort gained momentum a week after the storm, some 20,000 active-duty soldiers from all military branches were posted to Louisiana, Alabama and Mississippi under the command of Lt. Gen. Russel Honore, the towering Louisiana native in charge of Joint Task Force Katrina.

In the city's Lakeview neighborhood, the floodwaters still run deep two weeks after the hurricane, and looters are another persistent problem. Staff Sgt. Travis Sigfridson, of the 186th Infantry Regiment, patrols the area by airboat.

Firefighters attempt to crank up a small portable pump in a bid to keep a Columbus Street house fire from spreading in the 7th Ward. Helicopters dunked giant buckets into the Mississippi River and dumped them on the blaze, but to no avail.

A distraught Robert Fonteaine is able to rescue only his pup, Gangster, and a few tools from his home. Candles being used for illumination in a city without electricity were blamed for many of the post-Katrina house fires.

A geyser of inky black smoke rises over the Central City area. At first it seemed impossible that a sodden city would be beset by fire, but within a day of Katrina, buildings had been torched or accidentally set afire.

While the military sought to rescue survivors and clear the city of holdouts, some residents slipped back into their apartments. This man submits to frisking by New Orleans Police Capt. Bobby Norton, left, and officer Ronnie Stevens after they spotted him bicycling through Uptown New Orleans with a gun strapped to his side. Police accepted the man's explanation — that the weapon was for self-protection — and he was allowed to continue on his way.

ALEX BRANDON

CHRIS GRANGER

On a balcony in Algiers Point, resident Gary Stubbs catches a couple of hours of sleep as part of a self-appointed posse that guarded the neighborhood against looters. The weapons, including an AK-47 assault rifle, five shotguns, a derringer, a flare gun and a pistol, were donated by evacuees who had given the neighborhood defense force permission to enter their homes and take what they needed.

A Blackhawk helicopter hovers overhead as a paddler returns to the B.W. Cooper public housing development in a flatboat laden with bottled water.

ALEX BRANDON

On the front lines

Reporting the story of the century

GORDON RUSSELL
Times-Picayune reporter

While much of the first week after Katrina was infused with a sense of danger, Thursday, for me, was the day that felt like it was all over for New Orleans. The promised troops and buses had failed to materialize. The stores had been looted, and flood victims still trapped in the city were getting very jumpy. So were the cops.

That morning, I went out on my porch and saw a man trying to siphon gas from a neighbor's car — just enough to get out of the city, he said, before we ran him off. A few minutes later, I was helping an out-of-town photographer try to change a flat tire on his massive SUV when two scowling young men approached on foot, clearly with designs on the car. Just then a neighbor came over with a tire iron to help us. Outnumbered, the would-be hijackers moved on.

After talking to people still marooned in the reeking, sweltering Dome, the photographer, Marko Georgiev, and I drove over to the Convention Center. The unrest there was even more edgy. Young men were breaking into parked cars, and groups of desperate people eyed our gassed-up SUV with barely concealed lust. Sensing conditions were ripe for a riot, we took off, scooping up a young amateur photographer as we went, before he further antagonized people caught in the desperate conditions he was trying to document.

> **"YOUNG MEN WERE BREAKING INTO PARKED CARS, AND GROUPS OF DESPERATE PEOPLE EYED OUR GASSED-UP SUV WITH BARELY CONCEALED LUST. SENSING CONDITIONS WERE RIPE FOR A RIOT, WE TOOK OFF."**

As we drove away, up Tchoupitoulas Street, we saw what looked like the aftermath of a shootout. There was an RTA bus parked at an odd angle in the street, a limousine crashed into a lamppost, a group of cops shouldering rifles. A bloodied man lay face down on the pavement at their feet, apparently dead. I fought back a surge of nausea and scribbled some notes as Marko fired off a few exposures.

We had started to drive through the intersection when several cops yelled at us to stop. Sensing that Marko was tempted to gun the motor and make a run for it, I hollered at him: The cops had their guns trained on us. Now they rushed the car, pointing weapons at our heads. Cursing and shouting, they hauled us out of the SUV and pressed our faces into the wall of a building.

One cop grabbed Marko's camera and sent it skittering — despite, or perhaps because of, our protestations that we were journalists. Another went through my pockets, grabbed my notebook and threw it after Marko's camera. Every time I tried to get a word in, my face was pushed against the wall. But suddenly, Marko had his camera back, and they were yelling at us to go. When I told the police they had no right to confiscate my notebook, I was told to leave. A glance to the rear of the car revealed it was sitting on the bumper. I grabbed it and we split. The guy we had picked up was wide-eyed. He wanted to know if this was a typical interaction with the police in New Orleans. I said it wasn't. Nothing about Katrina was typical."

A Claiborne Avenue convoy of soldiers passes St. Louis Cemetery No. 2.

"NOW GET OFF YOUR ASSES AND LET'S DO SOMETHING. ... LET'S FIX THE BIGGEST GODDAMN CRISIS IN THE HISTORY OF THIS COUNTRY."

Mayor Ray Nagin to state and federal officials, Sept. 2

"I truly believed the White House was not at fault here."

Former FEMA chief Michael Brown, Sept. 14

"MIKE BROWN WASN'T ENGAGED THEN, AND HE SURELY ISN'T NOW. HE SHOULD HAVE BEEN WATCHING CNN INSTEAD OF THE DISNEY CHANNEL."

Gov. Kathleen Blanco spokeswoman Denise Bottcher, Sept. 28

"BROWNIE, YOU'RE DOING

"MY BIGGEST MISTAKE WAS NOT RECOGNIZING, BY SATURDAY, THAT LOUISIANA WAS DYSFUNCTIONAL."

Former FEMA chief Michael Brown, Sept. 25

"Funda- mentally the first break- down occurred at the local level."

A state official who works with FEMA, Sept. 2

"This is bureaucracy at its worst and this bureaucracy at its worst has committed murder in the New Orleans area."

Jefferson Parish President Aaron Broussard, Sept. 7

"Would the president please stop taking photo-ops, and please come and see what I'm trying to show him?"

U.S. Sen. Mary Landrieu, Sept. 4

A HECK OF A JOB."

'He's come from Washington and he's here to help us."

Gov. Kathleen Blanco, introducing Bush liaison Donald Powell, left, early December

THE BLAME GAME

WITHIN DAYS IT WAS CLEAR THAT THE POLITICAL DAMAGE FROM THE CATASTROPHE MIGHT RIVAL KATRINA'S TOLL ON THE CITY ITSELF, AND PUBLIC OFFICIALS BEGAN TURNING ON EACH OTHER IN EVER MORE FRANTIC ROUNDS OF FINGERPOINTING. Mayor Ray Nagin took to the airwaves to hurl salty castigations in the direction of state and federal officials, accusing them of preening before TV cameras when they should have been in the city leading the recovery. Critics later would blame Nagin himself for lack of leadership. Days after lauding FEMA boss Michael Brown for "a heck of a job," President Bush sacked the bureaucrat — who first blamed the failed FEMA relief effort on "dysfunctional" Louisiana politics and then decided his own boss, Homeland Security Secretary Michael Chertoff, was the real culprit. At the local level, a weepy Jefferson Parish President Aaron Broussard took flack for ordering pump workers to abandon their posts and evacuate to Washington Parish, a command that he publicly regretted a few months later. His own stab at the blame game was to assail East Jefferson Levee Board President Pat Bossetta for dereliction of duty during the storm and secure his removal by the governor. Underlying all of the political jousting were much more fundamental questions of accountability: Why had the federal levee system failed? And what must the Army Corps of Engineers do to keep it from happening again?

As helicopters rush off with the most desperately ill, throngs trapped for nearly a week in New Orleans climb aboard buses on Saturday afternoon, five days after Katrina made landfall.

CLEARING THE CITY

SUNDAY KATRINA: THE STORM WE'VE ALWAYS FEARED
The Times-Picayune

After five days, thousands of anguished
storm victims finally have a reason for hope

HELP AT LAST

Amid chaos, a rare voice of strength

Authorities regaining grip on city

ELIOT KAMENITZ

SEPT. 4, 2005

THE GOVERNMENT RESPONSE TO THE CATASTROPHE THAT WAS KATRINA FAILED IN COUNTLESS WAYS AND AT EVERY LEVEL OF AUTHORITY. Nursing homes weren't evacuated as they should have been. Shelters weren't properly equipped to receive the throngs who sought refuge in them. But one question cut to the very heart of the debacle: Where were the buses? Why did it take the better part of a week for the richest nation on earth to muster the rolling stock needed to rescue tens of thousands of New Orleanians from the misery they had endured for days on end in the Superdome and the Convention Center? Finally, as the weekend arrived, so did the armada of buses belatedly organized by FEMA. In short order, the Superdome and the Convention Center were cleared and so were the highway overpasses where boat rescuers had dropped off survivors before rushing back into a flooded city to continue the search. For some, the bus rides ended in Baton Rouge. Others pressed on to Texas and, in short order, the Astrodome was a more functional and sanitary version of the New Orleans encampments that finally had been broken up.

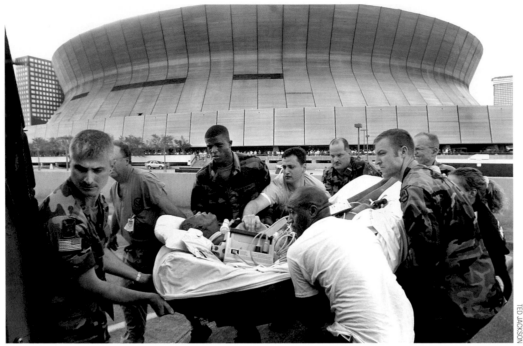

With the Superdome looming in the background, medics load a critically ill patient into a Blackhawk helicopter.

TED JACKSON

Baggage carts hold human cargo at Armstrong International Airport as evacuees are airlifted to cities across the nation.

BRETT DUKE

A week after the storm, New Orleans residents clamber out of a National Guard truck that has brought them to Stallings Gymnasium and Youth Center in the 9th Ward, a pick-up point for helicopters airlifting survivors from the flooded city.

By Friday, four days after the hurricane, Louis Armstrong International Airport is thronged with people rescued belatedly from the Superdome and Convention Center and awaiting flights to destinations across the breadth of the United States.

DAVID GRUNFELD

AP

The Houston Astrodome burgeons into an instant city after buses rumble across south Louisiana bearing survivors rescued from the horrors of a flooded New Orleans.

"I CAN'T SAY I'M GOING HOME.

I DON'T KNOW WHERE HOME IS

James Myles, now in Milwaukee, Wisconsin

KATHY ANDERSON

ANYM**O**RE."

THE DISPERSAL

CHRIS GRANGER

SOCIOLOGISTS IN SEARCH OF COMPARABLE DISLOCATIONS CAST BACK TO THE GREAT MID-CENTURY MIGRATION NORTH FROM THE MISSISSIPPI DELTA IN SEEKING TO UNDERSTAND THE CULTURAL IMPACT OF THE DIASPORA TRIGGERED BY KATRINA. Fifty states rolled out the welcome mat as suddenly homeless and sometimes bewildered Louisianians stepped off planes and buses in cities they had barely heard of. Homesickness — truly feeling the impact of the old lyric: "Do you know what it means to miss New Orleans?" — reached epidemic proportions. Partly as an antidote to their isolation, partly because New Orleanians would not have it any other way, local menus and music halls began to feel the presence of the newcomers, whose ranks included top chefs as well as funk and brass band artists. Mardi Gras mask makers turned up in Virginia. Etouffée became a popular feature among offerings at an Omaha pizza parlor after a transplanted cook introduced Nebraskans to the Creole classic. Like other students displaced to Houston's Scarsborough High School, Calvin Jones (inset) proudly sported Louisiana-themed dogtags. For James Myles, left, temporary relocation to Wisconsin included an introduction to something as exotic as anything the New Orleanians brought with them: snow.

"WE ARE NUMB. WE ARE DISMAYED. WE ARE LOCKED ONTO EVERY NATIONAL TELEVISION STATION, REMOTES IN HAND, AS WE FEEL THE NAUSEA THAT OVERCOMES US. WE ARE HOMELESS."

Betty Aasgaard-DeSchinckel, writing from Las Vegas, Sept. 20

CHRIS GRANGER

Lemoyne Reine, 21, found himself exiled by Katrina to an apartment in southwest Houston, unfurnished but for an air mattress that had sprung a leak.

"I DON'T HAVE NOBODY TO GO BACK TO. NOTHING. NOBODY. NO PLACE TO GO. BUT I DON'T HAVE ANYTHING TO STAY FOR EITHER."

Lemoyne Reine Jr., 21, in Houston

"I've talked bad about our city at times: the politics, the crime, the schools. I've said numerous times that if I could, I would live elsewhere. I'm eating those words."

Billie Sloss, writing from Harahan, Sept. 27

"THEY HAVE GOOD FOOD. IT'S JUST THAT I'M USED TO FOOD HAVING AN ATTITUDE, AND MILWAUKEE FOOD JUST DOESN'T HAVE THE ATTITUDE."

KATHY ANDERSON

James Myles, who started a catering company called Cajun Quizines after Katrina blew him to Milwaukee, regales guests at a Mardi Gras party at the Senior Resource Center in Shorewood, Wisc.

James Myles, now in Milwaukee, Wisconsin

"We aren't the ones you see on cots at the Astrodome. We aren't the ones you saw paddling to safety among the rooftops of a flooded city. Most of us didn't endure the despair of the Convention Center. We left the city before it became Hell on Earth — but **we only made it as far as Purgatory**."

Chuck Wallace, writing from Morehead City, N.C., Sept. 19

"One hundred years from now, someone will ask, 'How is it that Mardi Gras masks come from Norfolk?'"

GENEVIEVE ROSS/THE VIRGINIAN-PILOT

said of New Orleans mask makers Will and Kate Powers, who were evacuated to Virginia

"SOME PEOPLE LOOK AT US LIKE, 'OH, MY GOD. IS SHE REALLY BLACK?' IT SEEMS LIKE I'M THE ONLY BLACK IN MY NEIGHBORHOOD."

WHITNEY CURTIS

Tahira Lee, who was evacuated to Utah

"WHAT ARE WE RETURNING BACK TO?"

Former Orleans Parish public school system employee Clyde Robertson, confronting Mayor Ray Nagin at a town hall meeting for evacuees in Atlanta, in early December.

"THE BIG EASY IS NOT VERY EASY RIGHT NOW."

Mayor Ray Nagin at the town hall meeting

KATRINA'S EXODUS

The displaced survivors of Hurricane Katrina filed for disaster assistance with FEMA in nearly every county in every state. A look at the distribution of 1.36 million individual applicants who registered with the agency.

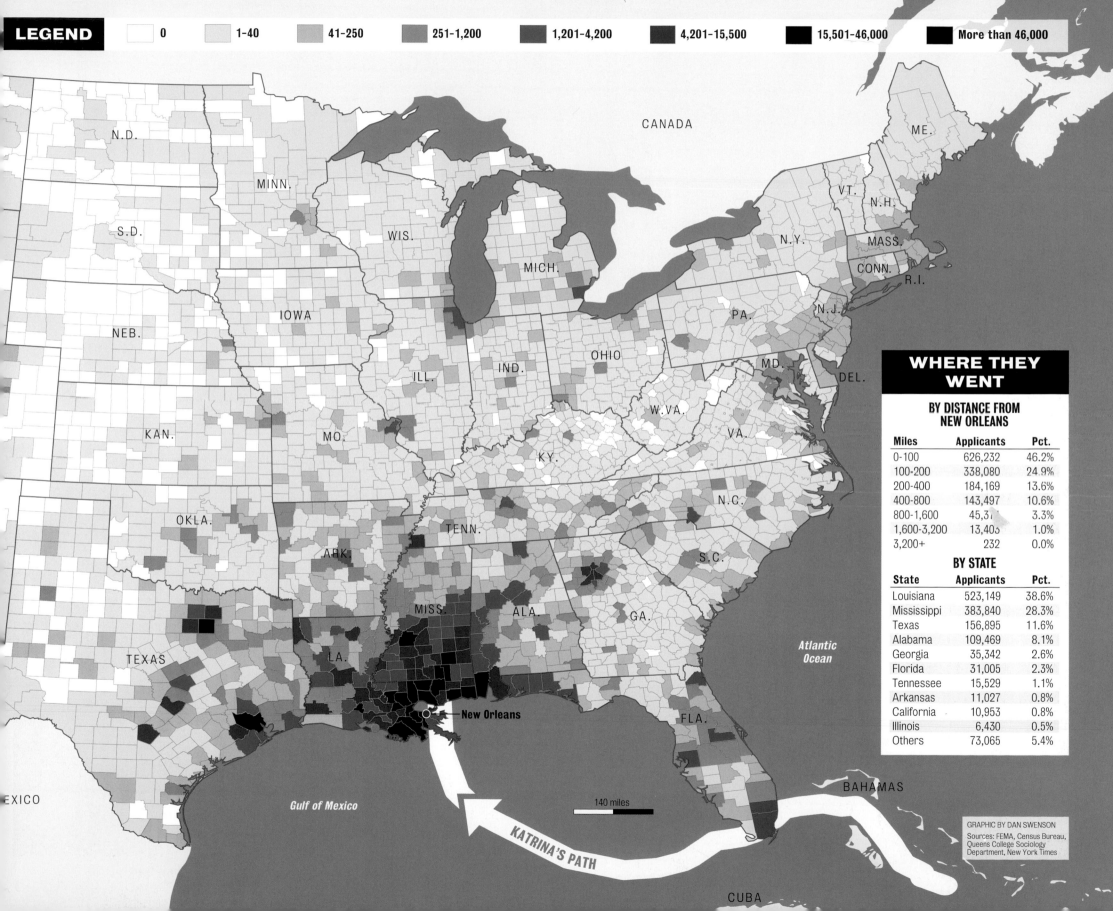

LEGEND

| 0 | 1-40 | 41-250 | 251-1,200 | 1,201-4,200 | 4,201-15,500 | 15,501-46,000 | More than 46,000 |

WHERE THEY WENT

BY DISTANCE FROM NEW ORLEANS

Miles	Applicants	Pct.
0-100	626,232	46.2%
100-200	338,080	24.9%
200-400	184,169	13.6%
400-800	143,497	10.6%
800-1,600	45,3??	3.3%
1,600-3,200	13,40?	1.0%
3,200+	232	0.0%

BY STATE

State	Applicants	Pct.
Louisiana	523,149	38.6%
Mississippi	383,840	28.3%
Texas	156,895	11.6%
Alabama	109,469	8.1%
Georgia	35,342	2.6%
Florida	31,005	2.3%
Tennessee	15,529	1.1%
Arkansas	11,027	0.8%
California	10,953	0.8%
Illinois	6,430	0.5%
Others	73,065	5.4%

New Orleans

KATRINA'S PATH

Gulf of Mexico

Atlantic Ocean

140 miles

CANADA

BAHAMAS

CUBA

GRAPHIC BY DAN SWENSON
Sources: FEMA, Census Bureau, Queens College Sociology Department, New York Times

Rescue workers' scribbled code records a grim tally
after a search at 2214 St. Roch Ave.: '1 dead in attic.'

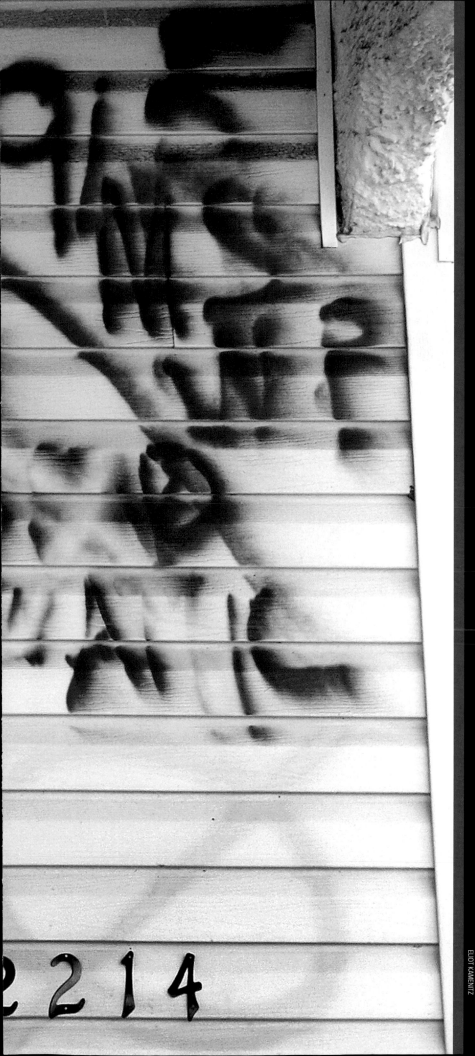

2214

1 DEAD IN ATTIC

KATRINA: THE STORM WE'VE ALWAYS FEARED

The Times-Picayune

DEATH TOLL MAY NOT BE AS HIGH AS FEARED

Before Katrina, there was Pam

SEPT. 10, 2005

WAS IT POSSIBLE TO LOSE MORE THAN A THOUSAND LIVES AND FEEL RELIEF? In the early hours after Katrina struck, the mayor on network TV had estimated a death toll north of 10,000. FEMA stocked up on body bags: 25,000 of them. There were ample grounds to expect the worst. Corpses were washing against the front of city buses as they attempted their last runs from flooding neighborhoods toward the Superdome late Monday. Before cell phone service collapsed, 911 emergency operators listened horror-struck to calls from residents trapped in their homes as floodwaters rose fatally. And a glance at shattered houses left no doubt that for some, death had come even more quickly. Initially, rescue teams had no choice but to ignore corpses in a frantic struggle to find survivors. Then began the house-to-house searches and the emergence of curious graffiti sprayed on buildings all across the city. Quadrants of a large X recorded the date, the affiliation of the search team and whether casualties — or survivors — had been found. The toll quickly rose above 1,000 and hovered there. But bodies were still turning up in the wreckage of demolished homes in early summer. As hurricane season 2006 rolled around, Katrina's death toll in Louisiana stood officially at 1,577.

DAVID GRUNFELD

New Mexico Guardsmen Saul Velez, left, and Anthony Broussard check a dislocated mobile home for victims during a sweep of Plaquemines Parish 10 days after the storm.

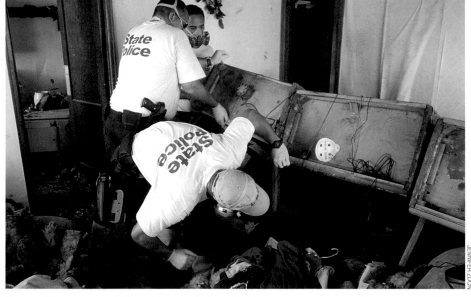
JENNIFER ZDON

The searching was thorough if not always timely. Six weeks after the storm, Louisiana state troopers, in a flood-ravaged Arabi home, are working through a list of 911 emergency calls that had gone unanswered as Katrina shredded southeast Louisiana.

Matt Sutherland with the South Carolina Emergency Response Team climbs out of a window after searching a home in the St. Bernard Parish community of Meraux.

The ubiquity of death did not diminish its horror. A storm victim is found face down in Bayou St. John, in New Orleans' Esplanade Ridge area.

BRETT DUKE

Violet Jackson waited 13 days before authorities removed the shrouded remains of her husband, Alcede, from the front porch of their home on Laurel Street in Uptown New Orleans. Far lengthier waits were in store for many of the families who suspected their loved ones were among the hundreds of corpses that were stored at the giant D-Mort (Disaster Mortuary Operational Response Team) facility that FEMA set up in St. Gabriel, outside Baton Rouge.

Dental X-rays are just one of the tools used to attempt identification of sometimes badly decomposed remains.

Survivors beseech D-MORT officials for information on a missing relative.

Relics of lives lost could be gently nostalgic or shockingly impersonal. Jane Estopinal ponders a piece of clothing that is among items left behind in the attic where her mother, Althea Lala, 76, died. Among other evidence of how Lala spent her final hours: a half-empty bottle of water, a container of Pringles and a burned candle.

About three dozen bodies were collected from St. Rita's Nursing Home in eastern St. Bernard Parish, which was swept by storm surge during the earliest hours of Katrina's attack. The failure of the home's operators to evacuate their wards led to criminal charges and a revision of state protocols applicable to nursing homes in the crosshairs of an approaching storm.

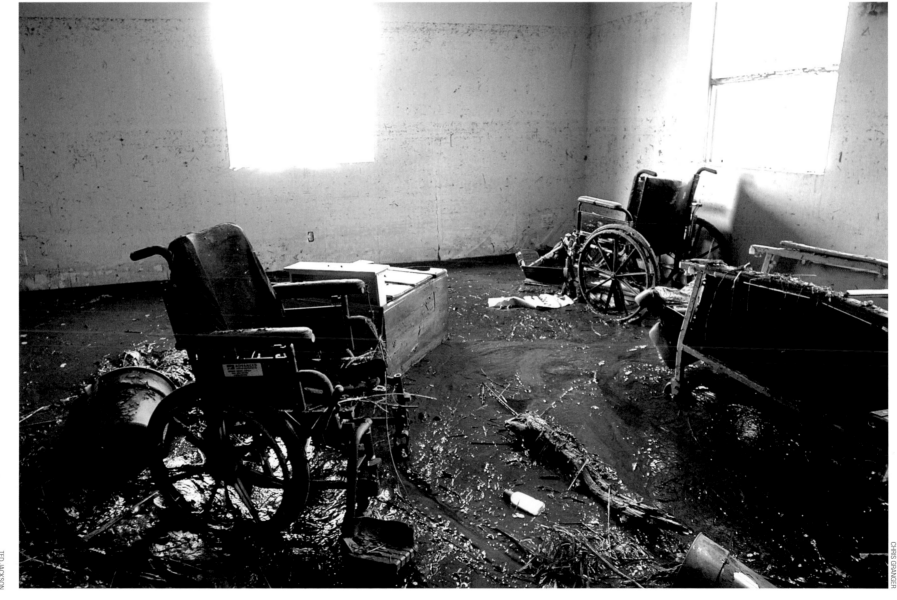

TED JACKSON

CHRIS GRANGER

95

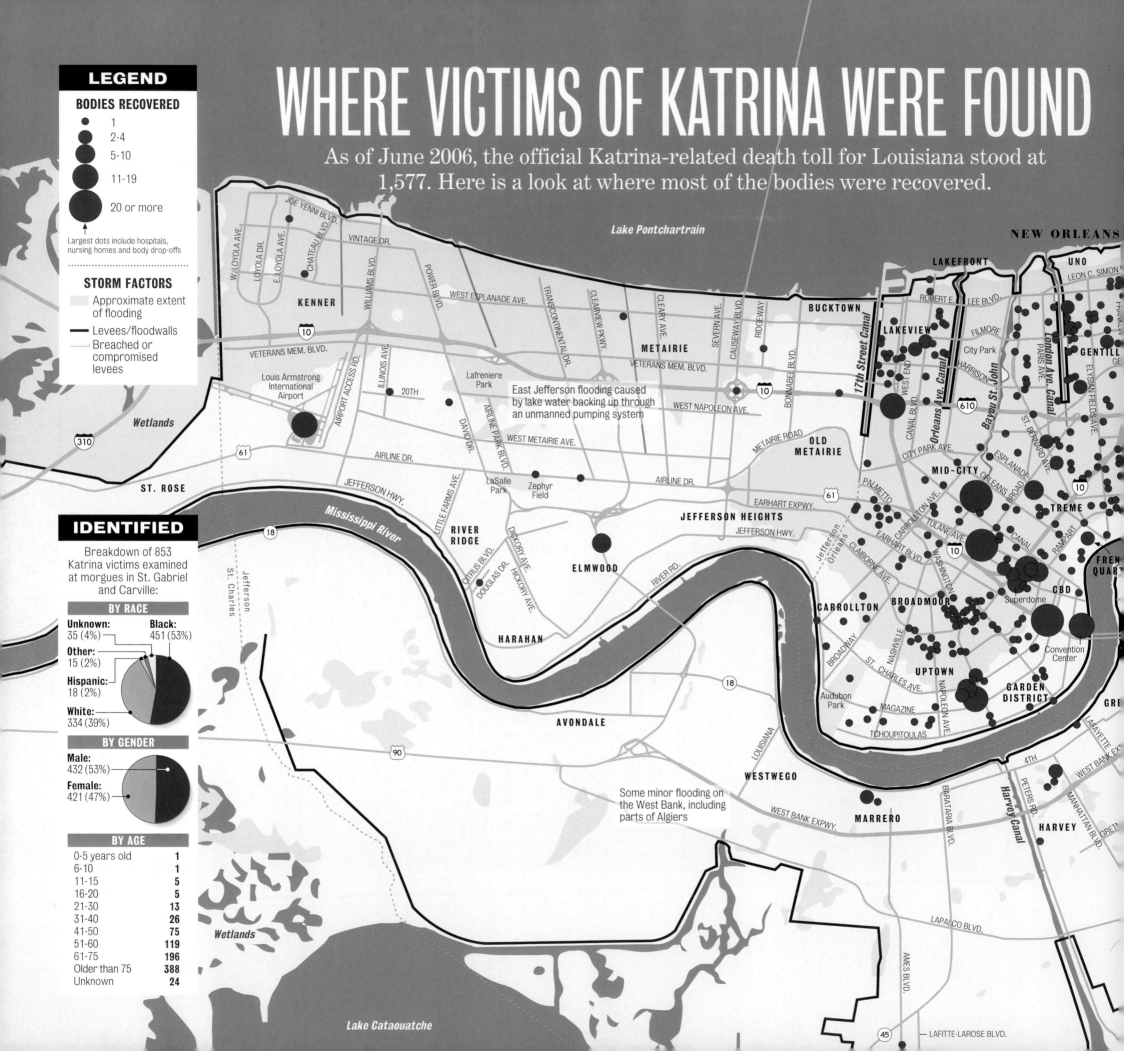

WHERE VICTIMS OF KATRINA WERE FOUND

As of June 2006, the official Katrina-related death toll for Louisiana stood at 1,577. Here is a look at where most of the bodies were recovered.

LEGEND

BODIES RECOVERED

- 1
- 2-4
- 5-10
- 11-19
- 20 or more

Largest dots include hospitals, nursing homes and body drop-offs

STORM FACTORS

- Approximate extent of flooding
- Levees/floodwalls
- Breached or compromised levees

IDENTIFIED

Breakdown of 853 Katrina victims examined at morgues in St. Gabriel and Carville:

BY RACE

Unknown: 35 (4%)
Other: 15 (2%)
Hispanic: 18 (2%)
White: 334 (39%)
Black: 451 (53%)

BY GENDER

Male: 432 (53%)
Female: 421 (47%)

BY AGE

0-5 years old	1
6-10	1
11-15	5
16-20	5
21-30	13
31-40	26
41-50	75
51-60	119
61-75	196
Older than 75	388
Unknown	24

Lake Pontchartrain

NEW ORLEANS

East Jefferson flooding caused by lake water backing up through an unmanned pumping system

Some minor flooding on the West Bank, including parts of Algiers

Lake Cataouatche

Map labels: W. LOYOLA AVE., LOYOLA DR., E. LOYOLA AVE., CHATEAU BLVD., JOE YENNI BLVD., VINTAGE DR., WILLIAMS BLVD., POWER BLVD., WEST ESPLANADE AVE., VETERANS MEM. BLVD., KENNER, CLEARVIEW PKWY., CLEARY AVE., SEVERN AVE., CAUSEWAY BLVD., RIDGEWAY, BUCKTOWN, METAIRIE, VETERANS MEM. BLVD., BONNABEL BLVD., WEST NAPOLEON AVE., LAKEFRONT, LAKEVIEW, FILMORE, City Park, ROBERT E. LEE BLVD., LEON C. SIMON, UNO, GENTILLY, PARIS AVE., ELYSIAN FIELDS AVE., Louis Armstrong International Airport, ILLINOIS AVE., 20TH, Lafreniere Park, AIRLINE PARK BLVD., DAVID DR., WEST METAIRIE AVE., Metairie Road, OLD METAIRIE, City Park Ave., HARRISON, CANAL BLVD., WEST END, Orleans Ave. Canal, Bayou St. John, ST. BERNARD AVE., AIRLINE DR., LaSalle Park, Zephyr Field, AIRLINE DR., JEFFERSON HEIGHTS, EARHART EXPWY., PALMETTO, MID-CITY, ORLEANS, ESPLANADE, Broad, TREME, JEFFERSON HWY., LITTLE FARMS AVE., CITRUS BLVD., DICKORY AVE., HICKORY AVE., DOUGLAS DR., ELMWOOD, RIVER RD., CARROLLTON AVE., TULANE AVE., Canal, RAMPART, CLAIBORNE AVE., EARHART BLVD., WASHINGTON, Wetlands, St. Rose, ST. CHARLES, Jefferson, Mississippi River, RIVER RIDGE, HARAHAN, AVONDALE, WESTWEGO, MARRERO, HARVEY, CARROLLTON, BROADMOOR, Superdome, CBD, FRENCH QUARTER, Convention Center, BROADWAY, NASHVILLE, ST. CHARLES AVE., NAPOLEON AVE., UPTOWN, GARDEN DISTRICT, Audubon Park, MAGAZINE, TCHOUPITOULAS, LOUISIANA, BARATARIA BLVD., Harvey Canal, PETERS RD., 4TH, WEST BANK EXPWY., MANHATTAN BLVD., GRETNA, LAPALCO BLVD., AMES BLVD., LAFITTE-LAROSE BLVD., Wetlands, 310, 61, 18, 90, 45, 10, 610

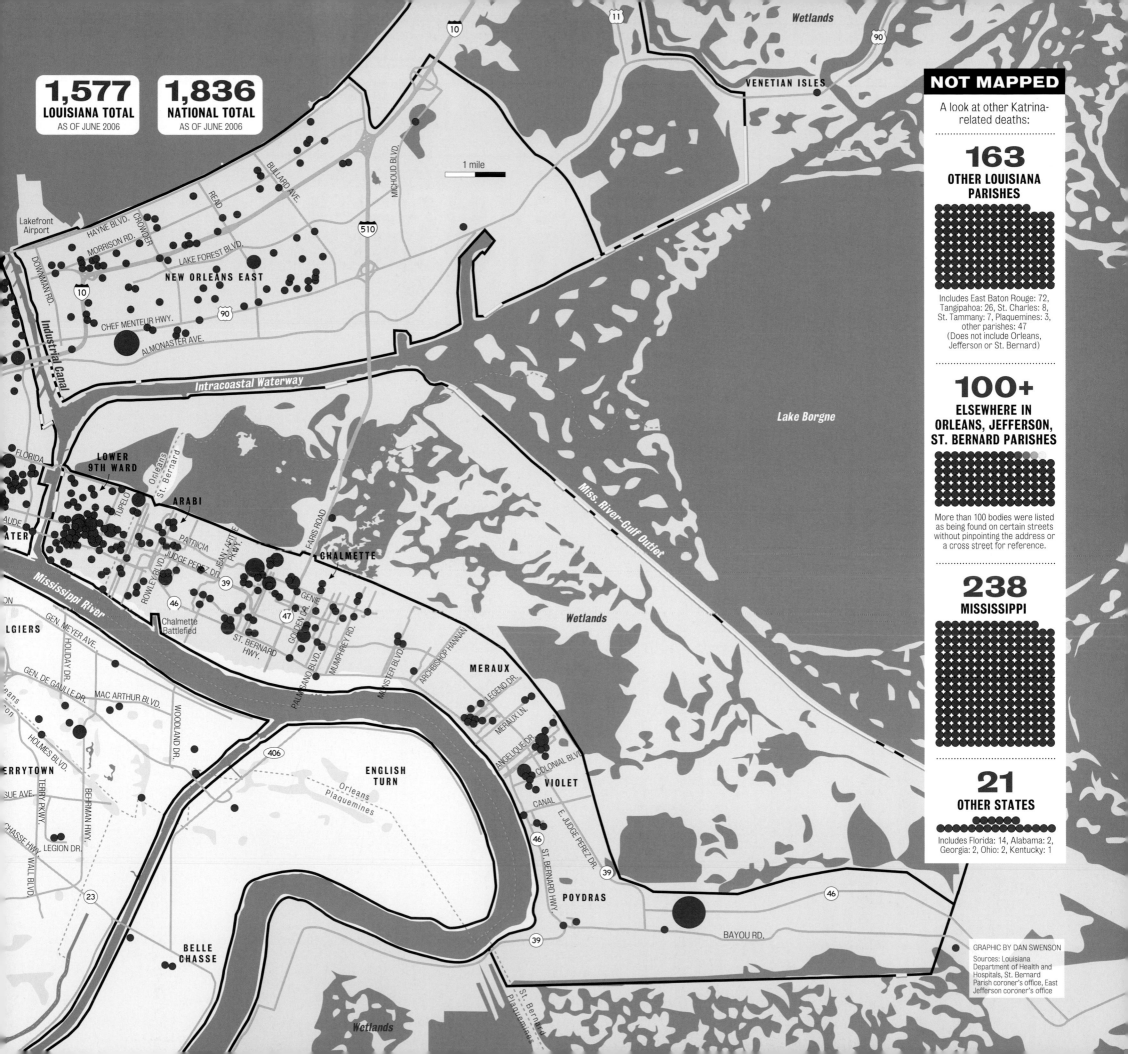

1,577 LOUISIANA TOTAL AS OF JUNE 2006

1,836 NATIONAL TOTAL AS OF JUNE 2006

1 mile

Lakefront Airport

HAYNE BLVD.
MORRISON RD.
CROWDER
READ
BULLARD AVE.
LAKE FOREST BLVD.
MICHOUD BLVD.
DOWNMAN RD.

NEW ORLEANS EAST

CHEF MENTEUR HWY.
ALMONASTER AVE.

Industrial Canal

Intracoastal Waterway

Lake Borgne

VENETIAN ISLES

Wetlands

Miss. River-Gulf Outlet

FLORIDA

LOWER 9TH WARD

TUPELO
Orleans
St. Bernard
ARABI
PATRICIA
JEAN LAFITTE PKWY.
JUDGE PEREZ DR.
ROWLEY BLVD.
FARIS ROAD
CHALMETTE
GENIE
Chalmette Battlefield
ST. BERNARD HWY.
GOLDEN DR.
PALMISANO BLVD.
MUMPHREY RD.
MUNSTER BLVD.
ARCHBISHOP HANNAN

Wetlands

MERAUX
LEGEND DR.
MERAUX LN.
ANGELIQUE DR.
COLONIAL BLVD.

VIOLET
CANAL
E. JUDGE PEREZ DR.
ST. BERNARD HWY.

POYDRAS

BAYOU RD.

Mississippi River

GEN. MEYER AVE.
HOLIDAY DR.
GEN. DE GAULLE DR.
MAC ARTHUR BLVD.
WOODLAND DR.

LGIERS

HOLMES BLVD.
ERRYTOWN
SUE AVE.
TERRY PKWY.
BEHRMAN HWY.
CHASSE HWY.
LEGION DR.
WALL BLVD.

ENGLISH TURN
Orleans
Plaquemines

BELLE CHASSE

St. Bernard
Plaquemines

Wetlands

GRAPHIC BY DAN SWENSON
Sources: Louisiana Department of Health and Hospitals, St. Bernard Parish coroner's office, East Jefferson coroner's office

NOT MAPPED

A look at other Katrina-related deaths:

163 OTHER LOUISIANA PARISHES

Includes East Baton Rouge: 72, Tangipahoa: 26, St. Charles: 8, St. Tammany: 7, Plaquemines: 3, other parishes: 47 (Does not include Orleans, Jefferson or St. Bernard)

100+ ELSEWHERE IN ORLEANS, JEFFERSON, ST. BERNARD PARISHES

More than 100 bodies were listed as being found on certain streets without pinpointing the address or a cross street for reference.

238 MISSISSIPPI

21 OTHER STATES

Includes Florida: 14, Alabama: 2, Georgia: 2, Ohio: 2, Kentucky: 1

"**THERE IS NO WAY TO IMAGINE** AMERICA WITHOUT NEW ORLEANS. **THIS GREAT CITY WILL RISE AGAIN.**"

President Bush,
September 15, 2005

WORTH SAVING

HOUSE SPEAKER DENNIS HASTERT COULD BE CALLED MANY THINGS — AND IN NEW ORLEANS HE WAS — BUT MEALY-MOUTHED WAS NOT ONE OF THEM. A city below sea level might not be worth saving, he offered, in blunt public comments two days after Katrina. The hefty Illinois Republican would later eat his words, but there was no denying that he spoke for many Americans. New Orleans might be the home of jazz and superb cuisine, of architectural treasures and the most distinctive regional culture in America, but there was no denying it occupied precarious geography. The city was outraged. The federal government had built the levees; it had a responsibility to repair them. If the Netherlands could defend itself from the sea, so could the richest and most powerful nation on earth. Two weeks later, President Bush eased local fears that Washington was prepared to consign New Orleans to history's trash can. His approval ratings in a nosedive as a result of the botched federal relief effort, Bush turned Jackson Square into a stage set for a national address that he clearly hoped would resonate like the stem-winder he delivered in Congress after the 9/11 terror attacks. His unequivocal support for the city's revival drew tears from the eyes of haggard and worried New Orleanians scattered to 50 states. It made for a great speech, though months would pass before New Orleans could be sure that the rhetoric would be followed by an equally resolute exercise of the presidential power necessary to wring vast sums of money from Congress.

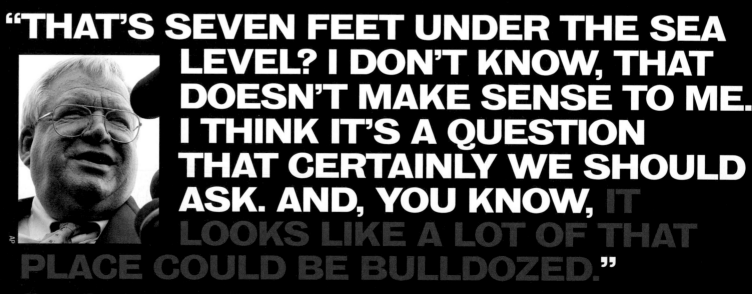

"THAT'S SEVEN FEET UNDER THE SEA LEVEL? I DON'T KNOW, THAT DOESN'T MAKE SENSE TO ME. I THINK IT'S A QUESTION THAT CERTAINLY WE SHOULD ASK. AND, YOU KNOW, IT LOOKS LIKE A LOT OF THAT PLACE COULD BE BULLDOZED."

House Speaker Dennis Hastert, August 31, 2005

THE RETURN

HELL HATH NO STENCH QUITE SO VILE AS A FREEZER FULL OF FOOD AFTER DAYS ON END WITHOUT ELECTRICAL POWER. That was a lesson New Orleanians learned over and over again — Rosalyn Herrera, left, among them — as they trickled back into the city to see what was left of the lives they had known before Katrina. When officials announced the first "look and leave" opportunity, a week after the storm, Derrick Williams, top, was among those who waited all night on Airline Highway in LaPlace. Herrera and her daughter Amy were among the lucky ones. Freezer aside, they found their Metairie home undamaged seven days after the hurricane. Others returned to no homes at all — just a pile of rubble or a slab swept clean of the house that once stood on it. The storm had not marked the end of the destruction. Isolated fires broke out as residents, or squatters, attempted to claim damaged structures. And then another force, as demoralizing as it was destructive, took hold: looters. An empty city with a diminished police force left scavengers with free rein. On a second trip home, residents would find upper floors that had survived the flood now picked clean of electronics, jewelry and other valuables.

Lesley Offner learned that her apartment in the Lower Garden District had survived the storm and flooding — only to watch on television a few days after the storm as it burned to the ground in a conflagration that firefighters were unable to fight for lack of water pressure in the hydrants. She returns to the scene on Sept. 18, resigned to her loss and determined to move on with her life.

Returning to Arabi in mid-September to discover that their homes have been destroyed, Laura Freeze sobs on the shoulder of fellow Arabi resident Angela Tyrone. The women are joined in prayer by Glenn Barras, associate pastor of Adullam Christian Fellowship, who also lost his Arabi home. Barras is clutching the arm of Derrick Young, a firefighter chaplain visiting from Seattle.

CHRIS GRANGER

In early October, newlyweds Paola and José Corrada collect what belongings they can as mold spreads over the interior of their first home together, on 35th Street in Lakeview.

KATHY ANDERSON

JOHN McCUSKER

AT LEFT, Eddie Zimmermann returned from Houston in early October to find that his house in Lakeview, all too close to the 17th Street Canal breach, was a total loss. It wasn't enough for Denise Godbolt, **FAR LEFT,** to lose a son in Iraq. On Oct. 12, she returned to her flooded and molding home in the 9th Ward and salvaged mementos of a young soldier's life: his uniform, his medals and the flag that had shrouded his casket.

CHRIS GRANGER

alter Goodwin hugs his neighbor Nancy Conerly as they run into each other for the first time since the storm, during a return to the Lower 9th Ward in December. Their homes were erased by the wall of water that rupted through the failed levees of the Industrial Canal.

Water rose over the roof of Gnann Cather's house on Paris Avenue, fast by the breach in the London Avenue Canal floodwalls. Masked against mold and dust, she returns in early October to salvage what little she could.

Terry and Wendy Borne rummage through what's left of their bedroom after Katrina tore the roof off their waterfront home in Venetian Isles, a community beyond the levee system at New Orleans' eastern end. "Everything we have is tied up in this house," Terry Borne cries.

Mold mottles the walls and mantel of a house on Burgundy Street in the city's Bywater district.

BRETT DUKE

GETTING THE WATER OUT

AT A GLANCE, THE MOBILE PUMPS, LEFT, LOOKED LIKE ALIEN CREATURES — mutant crabs, perhaps — crawling up out of the muck and murk of floodwaters pocketed under a railroad overpass along Franklin Avenue in the city's Gentilly neighborhood. The collapsed levees had been just the beginning of the catastrophe that befell New Orleans. In a city below sea level, every drop of rain — not to mention storm surge and treated sewage — must be pumped back out of the bowl brimmed by those levees. But in Katrina's aftermath, the city's infrastructure of giant pumping stations had also failed. Some were themselves flooded. Those that stayed dry could not function in a city without electricity. And so the Army Corps of Engineers and the municipal water board set to work draining the city — "dewatering" it, to use Army lingo. The first order of business was to plug the breached drainage canals, a task that took helicopters trailing giant sandbags that weighed more than 3 tons. The rest was left to pumps, both the portable kind and then, as they roared back into service, the giant screw pumps that had kept New Orleans relatively dry ever since the legendary Tulane University-trained engineer, A. Baldwin Wood, invented them nearly a century ago. By Oct. 11, after a brief setback when Hurricane Rita reflooded parts of the 9th Ward and with considerable assistance from the drought that was settling over the area, the job was done.

DRYING OUT

Because much of New Orleans is below sea level, floodwaters could not drain on their own. So, every drop had to be pumped out, taking more than a month. Most of St. Bernard Parish sits higher, so deliberate levee breaks helped get the water out in just a few weeks – until Hurricane Rita reflooded some areas.

Out-of-state technicians — Victor Anderson of Statesboro, Ga., and David Fulton of Wilmington, N.C. — worked in early September to clean and dry transformers at the city's flooded No. 6 pumping station. A behemoth, generally regarded as the most powerful pumping station on the planet, No. 6 feeds the 17th Street Canal.

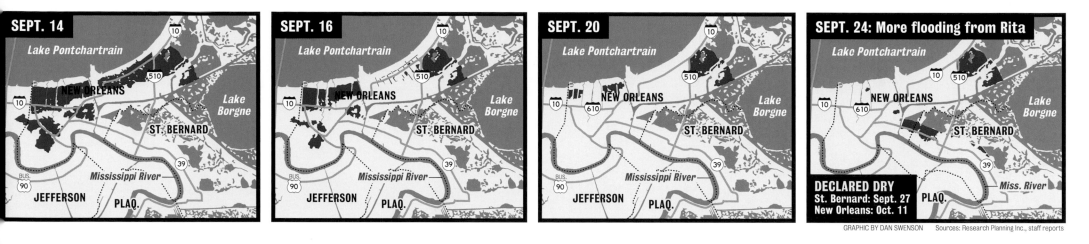

SEPT. 14	SEPT. 16	SEPT. 20	SEPT. 24: More flooding from Rita

DECLARED DRY
St. Bernard: Sept. 27
New Orleans: Oct. 11

GRAPHIC BY DAN SWENSON   Sources: Research Planning Inc., staff reports

The small Niagara Falls of water exiting Lakeview sluices under sound barriers and jams traffic on Interstate 10 near the Orleans-Jefferson parish line.

With the 17th Street Canal restored to a fragile functionality, portable pumps could hurl water into it from adjacent New Orleans neighborhoods.

Eleven days after Katrina, an Army UH-60 Blackhawk helicopter, **LEFT**, is still dropping huge sandbags into Gentilly floodwaters in a struggle to plug the London Avenue Canal.

109

REMOVING THE RUBBLE

HOUSES ROSE OFF THEIR FOUNDATIONS AND COLLAPSED INTO THE STREETS THEY HAD ONCE LINED. CARS FETCHED UP IN TREES. TREES CRASHED ONTO HOUSES. But more staggering than the weird and quirky patterns of destruction wrought by Katrina was the sheer volume of debris. With tens of thousands of houses still awaiting demolition and another storm season ahead, in early June FEMA could report removal of some 34 million cubic yards of Katrina debris, or enough to fill more than 1.6 million trash trucks. Placed end to end, the fleet of trucks would stretch be-

tween New York and California – three times. Removing the debris began quickly and proceeded erratically at staggering expense. More than $1 billion had been spent in New Orleans and its immediate suburbs within nine months of the storm. Contractors hired by FEMA and answering to the Army Corps of Engineers hauled the mess to consolidation points where it was loaded into dumptrucks for delivery to landfills all across the Gulf South. One of the larger piles was on the broad median between West End and Pontchartrain boulevards, left. Within a month of the storm it had risen mountainously high – the Lakeview Alps, one wag dubbed it – and then, almost as suddenly, was whisked away.

During a January 2006 visit to the city, the Ecumenical Patriarch Bartholomew, head of 250 million Eastern Orthodox Christians, picks his way across the Lower 9th Ward moonscape near the ruptured Industrial Canal.

A refrigerator on the roof, a clothes dryer buried in mud, a flipped car under a shattered house, a ripped-away door snagged in overhead wires: As these images attest, the capriciousness of the storm's destruction could be amusing, when it wasn't deadly.

113

Fallen trees were everywhere, some blocking streets and avenues, others impeding access to the houses they had damaged or crushed altogether. A guardsman clears fallen limbs from North Galvez Street in mid-September.

KATHY ANDERSON

KATHY ANDERSON

Ronald Lewis stands sentinel by the wreckage he has hauled out to the curb from his ruined house on Tupelo Street. **AT RIGHT**, the utter devastation of Chalmette makes for a colossal mound of debris off Paris Road, just north of the St. Bernard Parish seat.

TED JACKSON

Old Glory flies defiantly over a tattered, debris-strewn landscape surmounted by one of the few houses in lower Plaquemines Parish to have survived Katrina.

Flooded cars comprised one of the most lingering and obnoxious categories of storm debris. Some 200,000 of them remained in the city in June 2006, long enough to have become a campaign issue as Mayor Ray Nagin clawed his way back into the good graces of a scattered constituency and won re-election in late May.

The omnipresent debris and the graffiti it inspired became a fact of life in the post-Katrina world, too familiar to draw the attention of a bicyclist in Kenner's University City subdivision.

Refrigerators. Refrigerators adorned with slogans clever and
stupid. Refrigerators too vile for even the most
zealous graffiti artist to approach and besmirch. A quarter-
million of them, by FEMA's estimate, ruined in the flood or
utterly befouled by their rotting contents after the power failed.
You could call them the largest public art project in the city's
history, as one observer did — or you could call them a
godawful mess and wonder when they were going to get hauled
away. Whatever you called them, they emerged, unexpectedly, as
one of the most enduring symbols of Katrina, as familiar as fire
hydrants, more ubiquitous than parking meters.

SUSAN POAG

JENNIFER ZDON

JENNIFER ZDON

Refrigerators proved irresistible to sloganeers, many of them inclined to political commentary that ranged from salty to obscene. They also provided a good surface for the hasty advertising of services suddenly much in demand as New Orleans began to rebuild.

Within weeks of the storm, crews are hauling them off to junkyards.

Disposing of the refrigerators, stoves, washers, dryers and other appliances ruined in the flood — "white goods," in the jargon of the trade — amounted to an industry in itself. Refrigerators posed a particular challenge because so many of them were still filled with unspeakably vile foodstuffs, or the molds and maggots that had consumed the rotting foodstuffs and then, appetites unslaked, had set to work devouring the appliance itself. Hauled to junkyards, like the one along Almonaster Boulevard in eastern New Orleans, left, the refrigerators were first emptied by a grapple machine manned by workers wearing respirators and protective suits. EPA crews then evacuated hazardous chemicals such as freon from their cooling coils and oil from their compressors. After pressure washing, each refrigerator was crushed and then shredded to separate copper, aluminum and other recyclable metals. The residue was sent to landfills.

The water marks besmirch a grinning model on some advertising art strung up on a house in Lakeview.

The fecal brown stain was everywhere, usually well up on the walls of once-flooded buildings, a scummy souvenir that marked the upper reaches of the inundation that followed Katrina and the breaching of the levees.

MICHAEL DeMOCKER

ELLIS LUCIA

MICHAEL DeMOCKER

Runners in the annual Mardi Gras Marathon in February 2006 were treated to a somewhat more elaborate rendering of the floodwater's depth at the 12-mile mark on Banks Street.

BRETT DUKE

ABOVE LEFT, a homeowner on West End Boulevard offers a crash course on how to read the scum lines, which also adorned nearby electrical meters and a street sign.

Musical talent, even the riches that sometimes come with it, was no guarantee against suffering. Jazz and pop artists fled the cradle of jazz as Katrina bore down. The great concern was that, having found new opportunities in adopted cities, some might not be coming back.

Workers with the Louisiana State Museum attempt to salvage a signature white piano from the flooded Lower 9th Ward home of Fats Domino, **RIGHT**. Months earlier, Domino was rescued from the roof of his house by city and harbor police, **BELOW**, and deposited on the St. Claude Avenue bridge before being taken to the New Orleans Arena.

ALEX BRANDON

Photographed two days after the storm, a guitar and the blues legend's trademark black Cadillac are all that remain of the home of Clarence "Gatemouth" Brown, on U.S. 11 near Slidell. Brown, who fled to Orange, Texas, would die there 10 days after this photograph was taken.

SCOTT THRELKELD

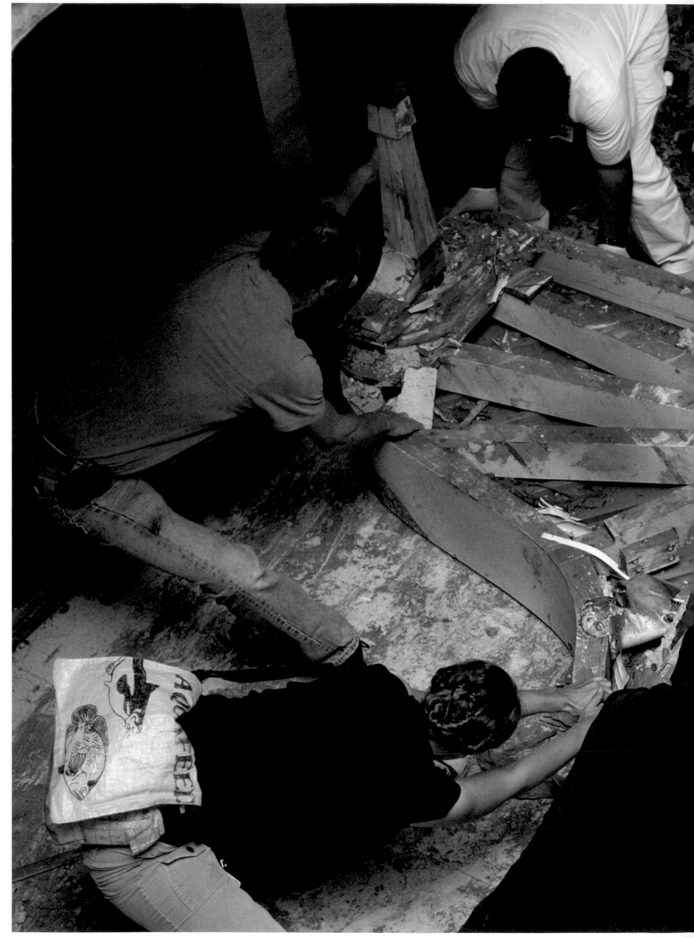

CHRIS GRANGER

ALEX BRANDON

Arriving on the Thursday after Katrina at the police command post set up at Harrah's New Orleans Casino, singer Charmaine Neville breaks down as she tells New Orleans Police Capt. Jeff Winn of an encounter with a rapist in a school building where she had taken refuge after her Bywater home went under water.

ELLIS LUCIA

Only the chandeliers remain in place as blind jazz pianist Henry Butler visits his gutted Gentilly home in early May.

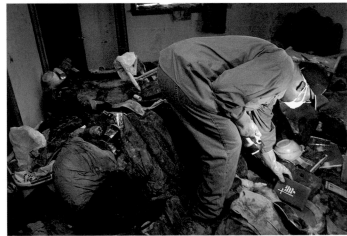

MATT ROSE

Traditional jazz artist and educator Michael White plucks a church hymnal from the debris during a late October return to his ruined home on Pratt Drive, fast by the breached London Avenue Canal.

125

LIFE IN THE RUINS

IT WAS STILL THE BIG EASY, BUT FOR THOSE BOLD ENOUGH TO RETURN EARLY FROM EVACUATION, THE LIVING WAS ANYTHING BUT. Jim and Terri Stuckey and their kids, Rachel, Sarah and Matthew, left, counted themselves fortunate to have an upstairs in their flood-ravaged Old Metairie home. They could repair there after dinner at a makeshift table they had set up in the garage off the gutted first floor. More typically, Katrina victims were lodged for a time in hotels or trailers — either their own or the ones eventually provided by FEMA. Police, firefighters and city workers took occupancy of luxurious cruise ships — two in New Orleans and one downriver in St. Bernard Parish — rented by the federal government at a cost many times what passengers would have paid to be plying the azure waters of the Caribbean, gourmet food included. But others, particularly in more rural areas, had to rough it: Tents cropped up on slabs where houses once stood. And for the least fortunate, there were the wrecked and abandoned cars, a legion of them that had been hauled to collection points below underpasses and bridge footings. The cars sat there more than half a year later, still streaked with brine and swill, their back seats caked with mud.

JENNIFER ZDON

For the likes of Donald and Colleen Bordelon, the lesson of Katrina is to take satisfaction in each other and in the meager possessions — drying out in their yard in Arabi — they still could claim.

Appalling loss could bring about a sense of angry despair, as evidenced in the sign posted on a gutted Lakeview house.

Sharon Morrow and Nita Hemeter dance for a moment to the sounds of Al "Carnival Time" Johnson blasting from Hemeter's car radio a month and a day after the storm. After that it was back to work: purging Morrow's house on Wilson Drive in Mid-City of flood-sodden furnishings and appliances.

Creature comforts also extended to domestic fowl. Feeding the chickens had always been a chore Maryann Russo attended to after she got home from work. The post-Katrina difference was that the barnyard where the fowl are feeding is the slab that underlay Russo's dining room before the hurricane pushed a tree onto the house she shares with Johnny Rancatore.

"I'D RATHER LIVE IN THIS TENT THAN LIVE SOMEWHERE WHERE THEY FEEL SORRY FOR ME. ...THIS IS ALL THAT I HAVE. THIS IS ALL I EVER OWNED."

Judy Morgan, St. Bernard Parish resident

RUSTY COSTANZA

SCOTT THRELKELD

Waiting for FEMA trailers, Judy Morgan and a friend, Cricket Livuadais, ride out the winter in tents set up on the slab where Morgan's home once stood in Florissant, a tiny settlement in lower St. Bernard Parish. With nighttime temperatures occasionally dropping below the freezing point, Morgan equips her tent with a heavy down sleeping bag and a kerosene lantern.

J.L. and Rosezan Giammanchere collected items from their destroyed home on Lakeview Drive near Slidell to create a shrine to the home taken from them by Hurricane Katrina.

131

REMEMBERING HOW TO MOURN

CHRIS ROSE
Times-Picayune columnist

Chris Rose had always been among The Times-Picayune's more popular columnists. Then came Katrina. Rarely has a journalist so deeply touched a newspaper's readership, augmented in this case by the vastly larger community of evacuees and lovers of the city who followed developments in New Orleans via the paper's Internet affiliate, nola.com. With his mix of humor, self-effacement and heart-on-the-sleeve reporting, Rose emerged as something like the conscience of a city on the brink. His e-mails burgeoned to thousands a week as viewers weighed in to thank him, to scold him, to share their own traumas and dreams for the city. The column that follows was published in early May 2005.

I have made the case that New Orleanians should take their out-of-town visitors on a Misery Tour so they would better understand what happened here.

I followed my own advice Saturday morning and brought two friends from California and my brother from Maryland – along with my three kids – to Gentilly and the Lower 9 for a look around before heading out to Jazzfest.

They'd already seen Lakeview and Mid-City the day before. More than anything else, the emptiness of it all is what stirs the soul. That's what tells this story. Eight months later, the question still hammers home: Where the hell is everybody?

While we were tooling around the 8th Ward, we turned up St. Roch Avenue and got stalled behind a gathering in the street and, unaware of what was going on, I backed up and took a circuitous route around St. Roch Cemetery and then ended up in front of the crowd.

It was a funeral. A jazz funeral, of all things.

It was small. A hearse, one limo and maybe 40 people following. Several men with matching T-shirts followed close behind the hearse, with their hands on the back of it and their heads bowed. A ragtag band played a slow dirge.

Unlike the big and brassy processions that follow the passings of famous musicians around here, this one was off the radar. It was just some family and friends and none of the attendant video and camera crews that can

"I SUSPECT MOST PEOPLE OUTSIDE OF NEW ORLEANS DON'T THINK THERE REALLY ARE SUCH THINGS AS JAZZ FUNERALS BUT HERE IT WAS, IN ITS LONESOME, WISTFUL REALITY."

turn these intimate gatherings into culture vulture documentaries rather than unique spiritual reckonings.

The St. Roch area is still so blown out and desolate that this pocket of humanity and color lent a haunting quality to the landscape. It looked like an apparition in the hushed grayness.

"Is this for real?" my guests asked me and I

told them yes, this is what happens here.

I felt intrusive – pulling over and opening the car doors for my guests – but how could you not stop and watch? I took off my hat, my one pathetic gesture of respect for those gathered, most of whom took no notice of us as they passed by.

As they turned a corner, the band shifted from mournful to mirthful – to that "Oh! Didn't He Ramble" sort of street jig they play when a jazz funeral turns its party switch on. And we watched from behind as the men cut, shuffled and buck-jumped and took their brother home sweet home glory hallelujah.

"It's like a movie," someone in our group said and that is indeed what it felt like. But real movies make events like these look so contrived and clownish that I suspect most people

outside of New Orleans don't think there really are such things as jazz funerals but here it was, in its lonesome, wistful reality.

This spectacle told my guests so much more than my words ever could, so I turned on WWOZ and headed for the Fair Grounds and we set about the business of celebrating the life and survival – albeit somewhat tenuous – of this profoundly soulful city and its culture.

And then this week, in a moment of down time, I rifled through some old papers stacked in my living room and found a death notice from last week announcing that a "Celebration of Life" would be held for Derrick Arthur Brown at Our Lady Star of the Sea Church on St. Roch Avenue last Saturday morning. And that's what we witnessed: a celebration of life.

I read more of the death notice and found out that Derrick Arthur Brown had graduated from McDonogh 35 and played football at Jackson State and used to mask with the Cherokee Hunters Mardi Gras Indian tribe

Mourners accompanied by the Hot 8 brass band parade through the streets of the city's Treme district on a Sunday afternoon in early October. The rite, remembering chef Austin Leslie, a storm casualty, revived the jazz funeral tradition for the first time in the post-Katrina era.

CHRIS GRANGER

nd was once employed by a place called B-
Neat Cleaners.

He was 47, with two daughters and three
randkids, when he died.

And it said this: "Derrick Arthur Brown
assed away on or about Aug. 29, 2005."

Eight months later, to the date, he was sent
o his final home and the measure of this infor-
nation leaves me stupefied.

What to say? We're still burying them. Still
urying us.

I don't have the words to comment on this,
o lend any clarity or perspective. It just sits in
our head with everything else.

Where was he all this time?

It fails to shock or stun because the bar on
hock value around here has been raised so
igh. It just is what it is. And if nothing else, we
nd in a back-of-town street on a cloudy Satur-
ay morning a small act of celebration, defi-
nce and closure for one more death in our
amily.

JENNIFER ZDON

By late September 2005, some 600 police officers, rescue workers and their families were calling the cruise ship Ecstasy home. Still others were living on the Sensation and the Holiday as part of a $192 million deal FEMA cut with Carnival Cruise Lines.

JENNIFER ZDON

Herbert Gettridge, 83, finds rather less elegant accommodations in the Lower 9th Ward home he was still rebuilding in April.

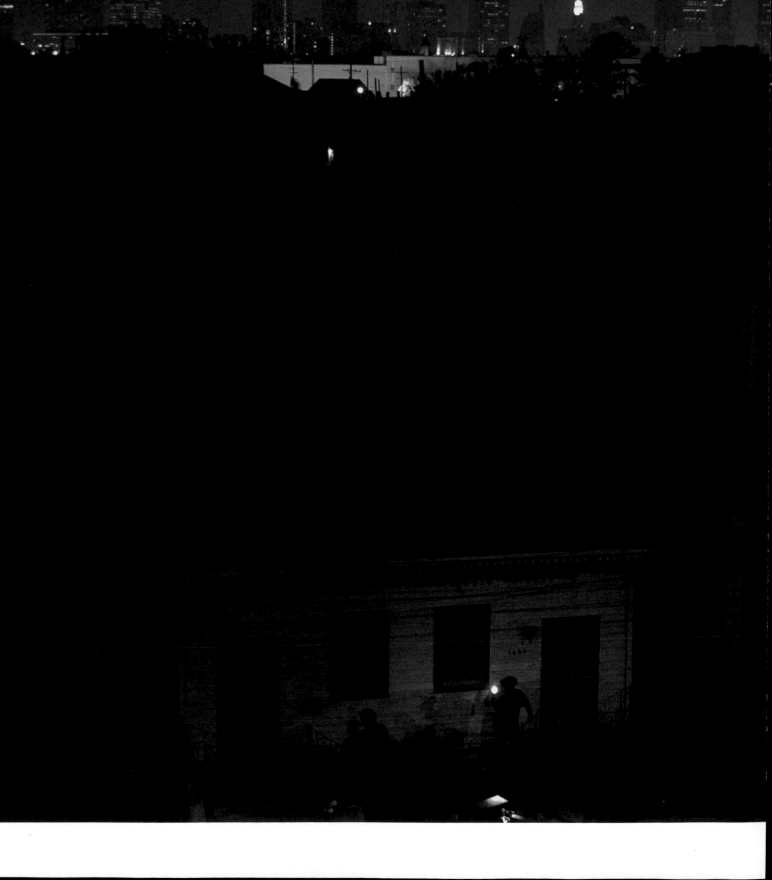

The pioneer spirit was never more sorely tested than after dark in a metropolis with limited electric service. A dozen weeks after the hurricane, power had not been restored to vast swaths of the city. Against the backdrop of the illuminated downtown area some two miles away, Jerome Rouzan and his family use a flashlight outside their house on Claiborne Avenue.

Power is not the problem for Slidell residents Ted Modica and Leann Hebert. They have enough of it to illuminate the fake palm trees on their patio off Rat's Nest Road. All they need is a house. For the time being, they make do with a motorhome, parked where their house once stood.

Uptown resident Joe Thompson uses Coleman lanterns to light the makeshift kitchen he has created on the second floor of his flooded home.

ST. BERNARD IS SAVAGED

THE ONLY THING MORE ASTONISHING THAN THE VIOLENCE OF KATRINA'S ASSAULT ON ST. BERNARD PARISH was the stalwart refusal of its people to give up hope. Of more than 25,000 residences in the parish, exactly five were unflooded. And most of the rest were, in fact, a total loss. Almost the entire parish government had found itself trapped for two days on a Chalmette rooftop as the storm surge flooded the parish to depths exceeding 12 feet. Horribly confounding efforts to drain and cleanse St.

Bernard, a giant refinery storage tank ruptured by Katrina spread oil over a neighborhood already fouled with sewage and swill. A crucifix (inset) cropped up in the middle of a thoroughfare, Paris Road, and seemed a fitting emblem for the community's ordeal. But with federal help — and in many instances without it — St. Bernard began to rebuild. When FEMA failed to come through with trailers, the parish scrounged up the money to buy them itself. When school aid was not forthcoming, the parish pieced together a St. Bernard Unified School for students of all ages from across the parish. Some of that same doughty resolve was apparent during Carnival. A new krewe, the Knights of Nemesis, left, made its debut on Feb. 19, a Sunday. Fifteen floats paraded down Judge Perez Drive — a brief moment of merriment in a very tough time.

Within hours of the hurricane, the Murphy tank farm, **LEFT,** is hemorrhaging oil. A month later, relief crews are still struggling to contain the seepage, which had coated roads and housing in a Meraux subdivision in the shadow of the refinery, **FAR LEFT.**

Parish officials bought their own trailers and set them up in Torres Park rather than wait any longer for the sluggish FEMA bureaucracy to deliver.

Brian Taylor, **FAR LEFT,** sits amid the ruins of his home in Yscloskey, after returning to the area from Slidell by boat, two weeks after storm surge tore the place apart. Many camps were lost, but those that survived were testament to the wisdom of raising structures at least a few feet above grade. Structures built on slabs, like the goner **AT LEFT,** had far less likelihood of surviving surge.

TED JACKSON

TED JACKSON

CHRIS GRANGER

At Bayou Bienvenue, near Chalmette, shrimpers take a break during efforts to salvage one of their boats, two months after Katrina decimated the commercial fleet.

Taxidermy drying out on a suburban lawn attests to the persistence of St. Bernard's rugged hunting culture, a legacy of its former glory as one of the most productive landscapes for fur trapping in all of North America.

CHRIS GRANGER

CHRIS GRANGER

CHRIS GRANGER

The fortitude and special character of St. Bernard were manifest throughout the long struggle to rebuild. **RIGHT,** parishioners of Our Lady of Lourdes Catholic Church in Violet walk past the ruins of homes along Colonial Boulevard as a Good Friday observance of the Stations of the Cross carries them from the river levee to their gutted sanctuary. Lang Shipley said she planted the garden, **ABOVE,** to take her mind off debris cluttering the Chalmette neighborhood where she and her husband, Peter, were rebuilding their home of five years.

Confusion and questions, manifest at an October meeting in the Parish Government Complex, quickly give way to action and results.

CHRIS GRANGER

JENNIFER ZDON

Many students had assumed the annual spring prom would be a casualty of the storm, but with donated gowns and a rented ballroom, juniors and seniors from the Unified School manage to bring it off in a downtown New Orleans hotel across from the Convention Center. For Dwight Richard, 17, that is something to celebrate.

144

Roughly 400 students show up on Monday, Nov. 14, as the St. Bernard Unified School opens for business in portable pre-fab buildings set up in the parking lot of Chalmette High School.

ST. TAMMANY RESURGENT

ST. TAMMANY PARISH, NEW ORLEANS' NEIGHBOR TO THE NORTH, DID NOT SUFFER CATASTROPHIC LEVEE BREACHES — only because there were no shoreline levees to breach. Remorselessly — and to devastating effect — Lake Pontchartrain swelled with water pushed in from the Gulf in a surge that topped out at 16 feet above the lake's normal level. Slidell was particularly hard hit, especially in the area of Eden Isles, Oak Harbor and Clipper Estates, left. Yachts, cars and then whole houses were tossed about in the swirling waters. But unlike New Orleans, St. Tammany lies above sea level — generally about 12 feet above, even in areas immediately adjacent to the lake — and as the tidal surge receded, the land quickly drained, sometimes bearing off as flotsam the homes it had so ruthlessly torn apart. A magnet for suburban development even before the storm, St. Tammany burgeoned only more vigorously as displaced families from New Orleans and St. Bernard took up temporary quarters on the north shore or plunked down their insurance money on a new house and made St. Tammany home. The repercussions were immediate and dramatic: crowded shopping plazas, booming businesses and traffic, traffic, traffic. A prestorm population of about 215,000 ballooned to an estimated 275,000 by year's end but had retreated to a more modest increase by late spring.

A motorist and his dog struggle toward higher ground after being stranded Aug. 29 along Interstate 10 near Oak Harbor.

In Slidell's Kingspoint subdivision, John Blank Jr. is helped away from a rescue boat by neighbor Donna Dallas a day after the storm struck. Within five days, **FAR LEFT**, a system of canals in the Oak Harbor area has reverted to its usual depth, but the waters are crusted with evidence of Katrina's destructive power.

 DAVID GRUNFELD

DAVID GRUNFELD

SCOTT THRELKELD

SCOTT THRELKELD

Carol Hess breaks into tears after getting bad news from an insurance adjuster at her home on Moonraker Drive near Slidell, two weeks after the hurricane. Shingles stripped away, **RIGHT**, a row of townhouses along Marina Drive in the Eden Isles subdivision sports FEMA roofs, the blue plastic tarpaulins that proliferated to become one of the icons of the post-Katrina era.

Before Katrina bore down on Louisiana, Albert McKeen had been bracing for the onset of a different ordeal: chemotherapy. In late September, **ABOVE**, he surveys the ruins of his home on Lakeview Drive. By early January, the St. Tammany School Board had deemed Salmen High School, **LEFT**, a lost cause and resolved to tear it down and build from scratch.

St. Tammany's rustic charm could also be its undoing. Falling trees, like those that crushed this house in Mandeville's Hunter Glen subdivision, proved destructive in many neighborhoods.

Pounding waves knocked apart the concrete fishing pier at Fontainebleau State Park along the Mandeville lakefront.

The ruins of the Piglet cabin are one measure of the devastation visited upon Camp Covington Girl Scout Camp. The Girl Scouts pledged proceeds from their annual cookie drive to a rebuilding fund for the camp.

Anastacio Cazu soda-blasts mold from a Habitat for Humanity house on South Street in Slidell as housing demand stiffens. **FAR RIGHT**, two of many transplants from areas more vulnerable to storms, former St. Bernard Parish residents Dawn Danese and daughter Christina, 12, admire their new home near Covington in late April.

SCOTT THRELKELD

By April, Richard Noggerth Sr. could stand tall among 40-foot pilings he had driven into his property on Rat's Nest Road near Slidell. He had decided to build his house 21 feet above sea level, 3 feet higher than FEMA advisories.

Storm surge having subsided, St. Tammany began grappling with a population surge. Far less seriously damaged than Orleans and the downriver parishes, St. Tammany became more than ever a magnet for outward migration from the city. Some of the newcomers would choose to make homes there permanently. Others moved in with friends or rented temporary quarters until homes in Orleans or St. Bernard could be rebuilt. The result was a booming local economy — and horrendous traffic jams like this one on U.S. 90 between Mandeville and Covington in late December.

Avery Estates residents throng the Slidell Library on Robert Boulevard to hear parish President Kevin Davis detail cleanup strategies in mid-October.

JEFFERSON BOUNCES BACK

THE FLOODWALLS ALONG THE WEST SIDE OF THE 17TH STREET CANAL WERE BUCKLING and beginning to fail early Monday when the east wall — the Orleans Parish side — collapsed, relieving the pressure that might otherwise have turned Jefferson Parish into a lake and spared New Orleans the horrors that lay ahead. But Jefferson did not survive Katrina unscathed.

From smashed glass towers, like the Galleria in Metairie (inset), to the twisted signs and roofless apartments that for months would greet traffic flowing in from the airport, Jefferson was daily reminded of just how close a call Katrina had made. By evacuating drainage pump operators,

as mandated under a hurricane "doomsday" plan, Jefferson officialdom instantly deprived the parish of the ability to keep ahead of Katrina's rainfall and the flooding that seeped in from Orleans Parish. Many neighborhoods were inundated, including the tony Northline area, home to some of Jefferson's wealthiest residents. At left, Henry Handelman came down from Jackson, Miss., to guard his parents' Northline home after they were evacuated by helicopter, eight days after the storm. "We will rebuild!" Handelman yelled from the balcony as he declined a ride from flatboat paddler Ray Rathle.

Glenda Nadions boosts her 8-year-old, Ryan, into an airboat in Kenner, **FAR RIGHT**. Karl Senner, 19, is on the receiving end of the Tuesday rescue effort. He and his father, Ralph Senner, and brother, Chris, are among volunteers with boats who flocked to the area to lend a hand. **RIGHT**, a young man empties a soggy boot after being rescued.

RUSTY COSTANZA

A week after the storm, Old Metairie is still under water as a group of homeowners along Atherton Drive use a johnboat and a truck and trailer to retrieve salvageable items from their flooded houses.

A day after the hurricane, Kenner police officer John Cusimano escorts a group of patients by truck from Kenner Regional Medical Center to Butch Duhe Playground.

Hours after Katrina's landfall, Catrone Henderson of Kenner rests in a tree after walking down Loyola Drive in search of an open store. More than a week later, Airline Drive, **LEFT**, is still impassable.

Like thousands of much more modest residences, a mansion on Falcon Street near the Metairie Country Club is tended from a travel trailer rigged up on an emergency basis.

TED JACKSON

Jennifer Duplain and friend Teresa Flannigan take a break from cleaning up floodwater in the Kenner home of Lloyd and Lauren Landry, Duplain's parents, a week after Katrina. The men pulling up sodden carpeting in the Landry house, **RIGHT**, are Duplain's husband and brother-in-law, Anthony and Harold Duplain Jr.

RUSTY COSTANZA

RUSTY COSTANZA

SUSAN POAG

Two weeks to the day after the hurricane, business owners were allowed back into Jefferson Parish as part of Operation Jefferson Jumpstart. **LEFT**, Dorignac's Food Center co-manager Mike Marchand, in hat, watches Scott Miller, the grocery's director of business operations, spray-paint a sign declaring the store's intention to 'open soon.' But emergency responders encamped in the Zephyr Field parking lot, **ABOVE**, and in the parking lot of the nearby Saints practice facility are hunkering down for the long haul. They include FEMA workers, fire departments from across the country, search and rescue teams as well as National Guard and Coast Guard deployments.

161

By early October, FEMA had rolled some 500 trailers into a field northwest of Baton Rouge and dubbed it Renaissance Village — the largest trailer encampment in the state.

TRAILER LIFE

KATRINA TRIGGERED WHAT MAY HAVE BEEN THE BIGGEST MIGRATION SINCE THE DUST BOWL, but for many of southeast Louisiana's latter-day "Okies" the trek ended quickly, not in California but in Baton Rouge — or, just as frequently, in the driveway alongside a flooded-out family home in Lakeview or eastern New Orleans. Icons of the recovery, FEMA travel trailers did not roll smoothly into the lives of residents they were supposed to house. First there seemed to be an unconscionable delay in getting them here, and local politicians could be heard bellowing loudly. Then many trailers sat in place for months before city inspectors approved the electrical hookups. By year's end, the trailers finally were available in large numbers — and suddenly local politicians were full of reasons why the trailers should go somewhere else, anywhere other than the parks and vacant lots within that particular council member's district. What remained consistent against this shifting political backdrop was the extraordinarily high cost of these temporary quarters. For trailers that had retailed at a little less than $20,000 before Katrina, FEMA was shelling out roughly $70,000, including installation costs and various service contracts.

SCOTT THRELKELD

JENNIFER ZDON

163

By late January, scores of trailers could be seen rolling into New Orleans, **RIGHT**, along tracks that parallel Hayne Boulevard near Lakefront Airport. Months earlier, indeed within two weeks of Katrina and long before the FEMA temporary housing began to arrive, Slidell resident Linda Williams, **ABOVE**, is able to enjoy lunch in her family's travel trailer parked alongside the remains of her devastated home.

SCOTT THRELKELD

CHRIS GRANGER

JOHN McCUSKER

CHRIS GRANGER

Mayor Ray Nagin at first stood up to City Council members and their not-in-my-backyard approach to trailer clusters. Then, in the face of mounting criticism from residents, he crawfished, accusing FEMA of high-handedness in moving trailers to sites approved by his own administration. Gov. Kathleen Blanco brought city politicians to heel, knocked some heads together and brokered an agreement that allowed the temporary housing program to continue — not without setbacks. The proximity of trailers to the fancy Lakewood Estates subdivision on the city's West Bank, **ABOVE**, led to a stepped-up effort by some residents to banish the temporary housing cluster. **AT LEFT**, Lakewood residents protesting the trailers argue the issue with New Orleans police.

For Kieyanna Magee, Chris Spencer and their three children, a one-bedroom FEMA trailer may be a cramped home — but it's better than no home at all. The family evacuated Magee's 9th Ward residence the day before the storm and eight months later is still holed up in temporary housing in Renaissance Village, outside Baton Rouge.

A resident checks the wall of mailboxes that serve her vast FEMA trailer complex outside Baton Rouge.

"THEY JUST KIDNAPPED THIS PARK FROM US. IT'S HAPPENING ALL OVER THE CITY. THEY'RE NOT DISCRIMINATING. THEY'RE TAKING EVERYBODY'S PARK."

Central City resident Bertrand Butler about A.L. Davis Park

Despite objections from neighborhood residents, trailers fill A.L. Davis Park, a New Orleans Recreation Department facility in low-income Central City.

he man with the rake is Buddy Lainhart, a Jefferson Parish worker who landed a trailer in the Elmwood strict after being flooded out of his home in Chalmette. "I consider this my home and I am maintaining it as y home," Lainhart said.

Tired of waiting for FEMA, frustrated St. Bernard Parish officials used parish funds to buy trailers and set them up in Torres Park, a green space also favored by ducks and geese. FEMA and the parish were still squabbling over reimbursement as hurricane season rolled around in June of 2006.

Renaissance Village resident Wanda Evans, right, gives a hug to chaplain Maria-Elena Sanchez Matherne during a visit by Matherne to trailer park residents in early October 2005.

Be it ever so humble: The home of the Rev. and Mrs. Cliff Nunn next to First Presbyterian Church of New Orleans on South Claiborne Avenue in Uptown New Orleans sports holiday touches as Christmas nears. Delivery of the FEMA trailer long preceded restoration of utility electricity, however. The Christmas lights are powered by a generator.

ATTENTION MUST BE PAID

AN EXTRAORDINARY ASPECT OF KATRINA WAS THE NEED TO CONVINCE THE WORLD — IN PARTICULAR THE PART OF IT BOUNDED BY THE WASHINGTON BELTWAY — THAT A CATASTROPHE REALLY HAD HAPPENED. And so the city's movers and shakers set to work, ferrying busloads of politicians and diplomats and visiting pooh-bahs into the disaster zone for an up-close inspection. Amid mounting criticism about the lackluster federal response to Katrina, President Bush had seen fit to cut short a vacation and touch down at the airport for a visit with state and city officials four days after Katrina made landfall. In late November, while the ambassador from the Netherlands to the United States, Boudewijn Van Eellennaam, left, got an eyeful of devastation adjacent to the breached 17th Street Canal, his seatmate, U.S. Sen. Mary Landrieu of Louisiana, yielded to a moment that seemed to mix exhaustion and deep dismay over vistas she had seen too many times. If many Washington politicians were laggards when it came to educating themselves about so costly a disaster, not so the army of volunteers who swept into New Orleans to assist in the recovery even before the city was pumped dry. College students on break, church-based groups motivated by a sense of religious duty, young activists nursing agendas for radical social change, they came for many reasons, but their energy converged in a remarkable singularity of purpose: gutting houses, feeding the hungry, treating the sick — often with greater efficiency than the government.

171

In early November, a tour of the Lower 9th Ward by Britain's Prince Charles includes the barge that crashed onto the streets below as the Industrial Canal's floodwalls failed.

U.S. Sen. Susan Collins of Maine, chairwoman of the Senate committee investigating the government response to Katrina, strides across a Mississippi beach with an entourage that includes Sens. Mary Landrieu and David Vitter, Gov. Kathleen Blanco, Mayor Ray Nagin and former Sen. John Breaux.

As New Orleans' vibrant movie production business cranks back into gear in early April 2006, actress Paula Patton takes time out from filming "Deja Vu" with co-star Denzel Washington to assist the Katrina Krewe, a volunteer effort committed to debris removal and other recovery efforts.

The Rev. Jesse Jackson surveys the wreckage of the Lower 9th Ward during an October visit.

TED JACKSON

CHRIS GRANGER

In December, former Presidents Clinton and Bush share a podium at the University of New Orleans to announce disbursement of money to damaged colleges from the Katrina Fund, a philanthropy they spearhead.

ELLIS LUCIA

Sen. Lisa Murkowski of Alaska, in coral jacket, meets with Lakeview residents at the corner of Fleur de Lis Drive and West Harrison Avenue on a tour of the area with Sen. Mary Landrieu.

"BY SEEING, THEY WILL UNDERSTAND WHAT HAS HAPPENED

Anne Milling, founder, Women of the Storm

MATT ROSE

A group calling itself Women of the Storm emerged as one of the more distinctive contributors to the city's revival. The activists' self-appointed task was to cajole, badger or otherwise persuade members of Congress to come to New Orleans to see firsthand how grievously the city had been laid waste by Katrina — and how badly it needed Washington's help. House Speaker Dennis Hastert, who had earlier questioned the wisdom of rebuilding New Orleans at all, is escorted into the Lower 9th Ward in March, **FAR LEFT**, along with Minority Leader Nancy Pelosi, in dark glasses, and U.S. Rep. Bill Jefferson of New Orleans, with head bowed. U.S. Sen. John McCain, the Arizona Republican, tours Lakeview neighborhoods near the 17th Street Canal, **LEFT**, a week later. On June 1, as the 2006 hurricane season began, the Women of the Storm, **BELOW**, gather in City Park to launch Storm Warning II, a campaign to dramatize the increased hazard to Louisiana from loss of coastal wetlands.

JOHN McCUSKER

JENNIFER ZDON

TO THIS CITY. A TELEVISION CLIP JUST DOESN'T DO IT."

The horrors inflicted by Katrina may have been sufficient to shatter the faith of the faint-hearted, but for thousands upon thousands of religiously inspired volunteers, the devastation was an opportunity and an obligation: to serve, to pray, to help a city heal. They came from all over the nation, an upwelling of the spirit as powerful as the storm that prompted it.

SUSAN POAG

JENNIFER ZDON

ABOVE, at St. Jerome Church in Kenner, Catholic Charities medical assistant Ileana Rotilan administers a tetanus and diphtheria shot to Evelyn Darby as others await medical care. **CENTER,** volunteers organized by RHINO — Rebuilding Hope in New Orleans, a program spearheaded by the St. Charles Avenue Presbyterian Church — go to work in January gutting the Lesseps Street home of Betty and John Chalaire in New Orleans' 9th Ward. Victory Fellowship, **FAR RIGHT**, a Metairie church, sets up a feeding station at Napoleon Avenue and South Saratoga Street in early October, one of numerous locations, including the Fellowship's home base on Airline Drive, from which the church fulfilled its mission to nourish the dispossessed.

CHRIS GRANGER

CHUCK COOK

TOP ROW, LEFT TO RIGHT, residents, volunteers and community activists press their hands against the repaired Industrial Canal floodwall during a Memorial Day ceremony in the Lower 9th Ward. College student volunteers encamped in City Park hold hands in a prayer circle before heading off to gut houses in mid-March. Pat and Robert Carter pause during work in November on their flooded Gentilly home to pray with members of Friedens Evangelical Church, of Port Washington, Wis., one of numerous groups that worked the streets of New Orleans offering spiritual succor.

KATHY ANDERSON

ALEX BRANDON

Howard University student Jacqueline Washington, gutting a house on Caffin Avenue in the Lower 9th Ward, is among thousands of college students who opted to spend spring break helping with the city's massive recovery effort.

As floodwaters receded, mold bloomed on rotting walls and ceilings, cabinets, furniture, beds and carpets. It came in a variety of colors and patterns, creating a weird, post-Katrina wallpaper that could almost have been called pretty, if it weren't so destructive.

MICHAEL DeMOCKER

KATHY ANDERSON

JOHN McCUSKER

MICHAEL DeMOCKER

KATHY ANDERSON

KATHY ANDERSON

FROM TOP LEFT, a children's magazine cover; a metal doorknob, evidently unreceptive to mold growth; a calendar still turned to August, the last month of the pre-Katrina era; a moldy latch on a chest; a silhouette against a moldy wall; a mold-encrusted souvenir photo taken on a birthday cruise.

Scores of volunteer and activist groups performed heroically in Katrina's aftermath. Two of the more remarkable were Habitat for Humanity, a group with long service in the construction of housing for low-income homeowners, and a newly minted, multiservice organization called Common Ground. The pre-fab house **AT RIGHT** was crafted in sections in New York City and assembled by Habitat in mid-December for Slidell resident Paulette Lindsey and her two children.

Anthony McGuay contributes "sweat equity" to a Habitat house under construction in Slidell while waiting for the organization to build his in Pearl River.

As June 2006 arrived — and with it the new hurricane season — Latin crooner Fredy Omar becomes one of the first to move into a village of houses that Habitat for Humanity committed to build on a tract of land in the 9th Ward to help house New Orleans' still far-flung community of musicians.

Common Ground was the inspiration of Algiers Point activist and sometime City Council candidate Malik Rahim. In short order it had become the focus of an international outpouring of philanthropic generosity, and initial programs to feed storm survivors in the immediate neighborhood had blossomed into citywide efforts to assist both flood victims and the influx of workers, many of them Hispanic, who had been swept into New Orleans on Katrina's tailwinds. Common Ground's blue-tented base of operations, **BELOW**, quickly emerges as a mainstay of the shattered Lower 9th Ward's attempted recovery. **LEFT**, volunteer Michelle Shin and Tamia Joseph, 4, stand quietly during an April 2006 vigil led by local ministers in the Lower 9th Ward.

CHRIS GRANGER

TED JACKSON

MATT ROSE

MICHAEL DeMOCKER

Common Ground founder Malik Rahim is mobbed by kindergarteners at Martin Behrman Elementary School in Algiers as volunteers arrive to distribute Christmas stockings filled with candy donated by Wisconsin schoolchildren.

n early November, volunteer Sophia Tintori from Brooklyn unpacks free lunches to be distributed to residents through Common Ground's relief center at the corner of North Robertson and Louisa streets in the Upper 9th Ward.

ELLIS LUCIA

JOHN McCUSKER

MICHAEL DEMOCKER

DAVID GRUNFELD

ALEX BRANDON

KATHY ANDERSON

SIGNS OF LIFE

THERE WAS A DEBATE: AMID SO MUCH SUFFERING AND WITH SO MANY NEW ORLEANIANS STILL DISPLACED, WAS IT APPROPRIATE TO BE CELEBRATING MARDI GRAS? The debate did not last long. New Orleans reverted to type and promptly yielded to the inevitable: Of course, we would celebrate Mardi Gras — as vigorously as possible — to show the world that we had survived, to show ourselves that we still know how to pass a good time. So it was that the revival of many customs long taken for granted became milestones on the road to recovery. The reopening of Slim Goodies Diner, top left, in mid-September — nothing but cheeseburgers and fries on the menu — was an early augury that the city might be coming back.

MOTHER'S NOW OPEN
Welcome Back New Orleans!

Mother's, the legendary po-boy joint, was up and running a month later. By late January, Xavier Prep, St. Augustine High School and St. Mary's Academy had pooled musical resources to form the MAX School Band, practicing, top right. The Mardi Gras Marathon, bottom center, carried a throng of runners through Jackson Square a few days later, and as Fat Tuesday rolled around, Juan Pardo of the Golden Comanche Mardi Gras Indian tribe, top center, had reason to smile. Triumphs came in big sizes and small. Bruce Springsteen's Jazzfest gig, bottom left, was a knockout. But it was just as important to the city's morale that springtime also saw West Bank youngsters scrambling on soccer fields, left, beneath a lightpole knocked out of kilter by Katrina.

183

AT WAR WITH WATER

MONTHS WOULD PASS BEFORE THE ARMY CORPS OF ENGINEERS ACKNOWL-EDGED THAT THE LEVEES HAD FAILED, not because Katrina was a bigger storm than they were designed to handle — the corps' initial stance — but because the designs were fundamentally flawed. For Col. Lewis Setliff III, that was a debate best left to theoreticians and spin doctors. As commander of Task Force Guardian, he had more practical challenges to attend to. Within weeks of Katrina, Setliff was working 18-hour days to shore up the region's fractured flood defense ahead of the June 1 start of the 2006 hurricane season. There were floodgates to erect at the mouths of the outfall canals, miles of sheet piling to pound into the uneven soils underlying too much of the levee system, floodwalls to armor with concrete splash pads to prevent the scouring that had led to collapse. And then there were the places — miles long at their worst — where the levee had simply washed away and had to be rebuilt from scratch. The costs were staggering. An initial $1 billion was quickly spent, requiring allocation of another $3.7 billion in June. Even those sums did not cover the projected cost of rebuilding the Plaquemines Parish flood defense — not to mention the all-around reinforcements that would be needed to protect New Orleans from the truly horrific Category 5 hurricanes that are said to be ever more likely in an age of global warming and rising seas.

Contractors armor the reconstructed Industrial Canal with concrete embankments so the levee won't wash away in the event floodwalls are overtopped. **RIGHT,** early May found contractors rushing to complete floodgates where the Orleans Avenue drainage canal empties into Lake Pontchartrain.

As the corps rushed to patch the levees back together, scientists and engineers played detective, probing for the causes of the disaster. University of California, Berkeley, professor Robert Bea, in bush hat, **LEFT**, ponders a failed floodwall on the west side of the London Avenue Canal near Pratt Drive in early October. Bea was part of the National Science Foundation forensic team led by his Berkeley engineering colleague Ray Seed. The NSF group found a natural ally in Ivor van Heerden, **BELOW**, the deputy director of Louisiana State University's Hurricane Center. Van Heerden's exacting computer models of Hurricane Katrina provided early evidence that storm surge heights were not sufficient to explain the floodwall failures and levee breaches.

ELLIS LUCIA

JOHN McCUSKER

Task Force Guardian commander Col. Lewis Setliff III scans the Industrial Canal by helicopter in mid-November. The barge that thundered through the breached floodwall is visible in the background.

The Jefferson Parish side of the 17th Street Canal provides a vantage point on reconstruction of the breached levees — for those who could find a way to see over the floodwalls.

For weeks, relief workers scoured the city for corpses, marking each searched house with a spray-painted X. Typically, one quadrant of this grim and enduring iconography would contain the date of the search, another the name of the agency that conducted the search. The bottom quadrant at right records the search results: 1 person found dead.

TED JACKSON

ALEX BRANDON

ELLIS LUCIA

LIVES LOST

Wayne Aaslestad, 64 • Bertha Acosta, 85 • Estrella Alexander, 76 • Dale Alexander, 55 • Peggy Alferez, 78 • Cecile Alexis, 92 • Hollis Alford, 66 • James Allen, 72 • Evelyn Ancar, 74 • Brenda Andrews, 51 • Ferdinand Andrews, 87 • Ruby Anthony, 75 • Irma Arcement, 75 • Betty Arceneaux, 65 • Douglas Arceneaux, 69 • Gregory Archer, 39 • Jose Ares, 83 • Lydia Armstrong, 89 • James Arnold, 87 • Rosemary Ashbey, 83 • Frank Ashley, 81 • Edna Asmore, 82 • Gertrude August, 84 • Joseph August, 82 • Theresa Augustin, 90 • Winona Austin, 80 • Beverly Babin, 82 • Justin Babin, Jr, 68 • Frank Bacino, 82 • Della Badeaux • Christiana Baham, 71 • Warren Baham, 82 • Earl Balthazar, 72 • Joseph Banks, 81 • Lillian Banta, 88 • Walter Barcellona, 62 • Samuel Barnes, 73 • Arthur Batieste Jr, 78 • Lawrence Batiste, 84 • Shirley Batiste, 73 • Irene Baulden, 79 • George Baumgartner, 95 • William Baxter, 60 • Ella Beard, 94 • Sonia Beard, 50 • Arzell Beason, Sr, 78 • Gladys Beatty, 84 • Mary Benjamin, 63 • Nercile Brenjamin, 82 • Sterling Benjamin, 38 • Carmen Bennett, 56 • Edith Bennett, 84 • Harry Berger, 84 • Carol Betzer, 72 • Inez Bilich, 87 • Joan Blackwell, 76 • Herbert Blanchard, 82 • Lawrence Blancher, 79 • Marjorie Blancher, 80 • Gloria Blappert, 81 • Nettie Blutcher, 94 • Gloria Bohnet, 80 • Anna Mae Bonono, 85 • Luke Bonono, 80 • Willie Boone, 80 • Errol Borges, 64 • Samuel Borne, 73 • Sarah Bosarge, 81 • Bulah Boss, 51 • Joe Lynn Bourgeois, 57 • Rayfield Bournes, 54 • Xavier Bowie, 57 • Gloria Bowser, 81 • Arthur Boyd, 48 • Loretta Boyd, 77 • Eugenie Boyle, 40 • Eunice Breaux, 76 • Helen Breckenridge, 77 • Chris Bridges, 34 • Johnny Brinston, 67 • Joseph Brossette, 81 • Alma Brouchard, 83 • Mabel Brouwer, 70 • Gerald Brown, 48 • Laurence Brown, 79 • Roosevelt Brown, 78 • Danny Brumfield, Sr., 45 • Mattie Brumfield, 70 • Selina Buckner, 97 • Lloyd Buras, 92 • Jannie Burgess, 79 • Mary Burke, 81 • Thomas Burke, 48 • Evelyn Burns, 97 • Winnie Burns, 91 • Owen Buse, 68 • Alex Butler, 68 • Benny Butler, 72 • Leroy Butler, 59 • June Byrd, 72 • Benilda Caixeta, 55 • Frank Caliste, 81 • Joseph Campieri, 88 • Patsy Capetillo, 94 • Claude Carpenter, 61 • Nathaniel Carson, 49 • Joseph Casamento, 80 • James Casby, 52 • Louise Casimire, 83 • Issac Castle, 58 • Irma Cevasco, 74 • Frank Chambers, 72 • Donald Charles, 2 • Onelia Cherrie, 91 • Ricky Chester, 45 • Warren Clifton, 71 • Arnecker Coleman, 35 • Darrel Coleman, 54 • Johnnie Coleman, 76 • Thomas Coleman, 80 • Ethel Collins, 85 • Lylton Collins, 60 • Guy Comes, 91 • Clarence Common, 85 • Wilmer Cooley, 80 • Myrtle Cook, 58 • Walter Cosse, 30 • Donna Cotham, 41 • Adele Cousins, 81 • Barry Cowsill, 50 • Ned Couvillion, 53 • Frances Cox, 77 • Ronald Cox, 72 • George Cronan, 74 • Mary Cronan, 78 • Wessie Crutchfield, 73 • Norman Cummings, 75 • Nicholas Cuquet, 79 • Stella Dabon, 68 • Frank D'Arcangelo, 66 • Irene Daigle, 83 • Amelie Dalier, 81 • Kan Thi Dang, 95 • Mary Darsam, 83 • Calvin Davis, 77 • Donise Davis, 28 • George Davis, 69 • John Davis, 59 • Rosemary Davis, 78 • Tanner Davis, 84 • Elaine Dawson, 59 • Duffey Day, 72 • William Deadman, 71 • Ella Deamer, 72 • Leslie Deamer, 92 • Herman Dear, 57 • Elva Deblanc, 92 • Evangeline Decour, 76 • Clinton Dees, 60 • Robert Delafosse, 39 • Zerelda Delatte, 72 • Alan Delaune, 51 • John Deluca, 77 • Jane Denley, 80 • Maggie Dennis, 89 • Agnes Depascual, 81 • Robert Dexter, Jr., 63 • Lawrence Dickerson, 22 • Milton Dieck, 85 • Roger Dimarbro, 63 • Blanche Dinwiddie, 71 • Kerney Dorsey, 85 • Katie Dreher, 90 • Rita Drury, 49 • Margaret Ducre, 82 • David Dubuc, 44 • Ethel Dugar, 61 • Edward Dugas, 80 • Harrison Duhon, 84 • Septeme Duhon, 68 • John Dunn, 49 • Harold Dupas, 77 • Gladys Dupor, 51 • Lorraine Duve, 79 • Mary Dyer, 72 • Patsy Eaton, 58 • Kemron Ebanks, 74 • Harry Edwards, 64 • Joseph Edwards, 45 • Lorraine Edwards, 58 • Marjorie Edwards, 85 • Clementine Eleby, 78 • Amelia Ellis, 71 • Russell Embry, 54 • Joan Emerson, 57 • Robert England, 56 • Michael Estarlich, 80 • Edward Ester, 76 • Feado Ester, 87 • Gregory Estes, 35 • Daniel Evans, 86 • Louis Evans Jr., 47 • Emmett Everett, 61 • Tesfalidet Ewale, 66 • Helen Fahrenholtz, 91 • Michael Falcone, 56 • George Falley, 90 • Shirley Mae Falley, 73 • Ervin Farzande, 44 • John Farzande, 48 • Alvin Fazande, 78 • Bernadette Fazande, 78 • Shelly Ferguson, 50 • Clarence Flemming, 64 • Prosper Flint, 77 • Alma Ford, 46 • Hubert Forrest, 86 • Ella Francis, 94 • Benjamin Francois, 99 • Ruby Frazier, 76 • Ethel Freeman, 91 • Maxine Frischertz, 84 • Caroline Fuhrmann, 92 • Robert Funk, 60 • Eddie Gabriel, 95 • Charles Gagliano, 81 • Shirley Gagliano, 71 • Wallace Gaillourd, 76 • Arthur Galatas, Jr, 81 • Tufanio Gallodoro, 82 • Mario Gardener, 54 • Marguerite Garr, 88 • Ellery Gastinell, 45 • Ruby Gauthier, 80 • Shirley Gayle, 73 • Robert Gibson, 85 • Ernest Gilmore, 51 • Arthur Ginart • Vincent Giuffre, 87 • Catherine Godwin, 61 • Thelma Godwin, 81 • Preston Goffner, 59 • Dulce Maria Gonzalez, 80 • Maria Delos Angeles Gonzalez, 52 • Rosa Gonzalez, 74 • Mary Gordon, 51 • Mary Gourgues, 81 • Marcus Grant, 57 • David Greathouse, 48 • Joyce Green, 73 • Marion Green, 69 • Rita Green, 84 • Shanai Green, 3 • William Gregg, 76 • Lorraine Griffith, 64 • Ayrie Grimes, 93 • George Grunik, 72 • John Gueydan, 81 • Robert Guillory, 51 • Goldie Gulledge, 91 • Charles Gulotta, 74 • Dorothy Gulotta, 63 • Ura Gurtner, 85 • Gertrude Hackett, 69 • Gilda Hains, 50 • Azemo Hall, 78 • Carrie Hall, 78 • Raymond Hall, 89 • Mary Hamilton, 79 • Iris Hardeman, 51 • Rosa Harold, 65 • Pearl Harris, 100 • Rudulph Harris, 73 • Martha Hart, 64 • Shirley Hartdegend, 78 • Oliver Harvey, 100 • Mary Hawkins, 78 • Paul Haynes, 78 • Mattie Haywood, 85 • Isabelle Hebert, 52 • Wilbur Hebert, 67 • Edmond Henry, 97 • Gladys Henry, 83 • Janice Henry, 53 • Thomas Henry, 55 • Ethel Herbert, 82 • Rosemary Herndon, 75 • Norris Heyl, 79 • Jules Hilborn, 86 • Kendrick Hill, 31 • Kevin Hilliard, 43 • Celeste Hingle, 85 • Dorothy Hingle, 83 • Gary Hingle, 51 • Audrey Hinkel, 72 • Dorothy Holland, 80 • Dorothy Holloman, 68 • Delia Holloway, 82 • Vincent Holmes, 47 • Alma Holton, 95 • Amelia Hose, 102 • Bonafacia Hotard, 77 • Lethea Howard, 57 • John Howley, 44 • George Huard, 91 • Adella Humphrey, 89 • Daisy Humphrey, 89 • Lloyd Humphrey, 93 • Herman Husband, 47 • George Hutcherson, Jr., 78 • Daryl Hymel, 50 • Edgar Hymel, 50 • Alice Hutzler, 90 • Robert Jachim, 83 • Karnettia Jacko, 26 • Alcede Jackson, 83 • Ann Jackson, 90 • Eddie Jackson, 97 • Elizabeth Jackson, 81 • Emelda Jackson, 78 • Ernestine Jackson, 64 • Gladys Jackson, 95 • James Jackson, 75 • James Jackson, 47 • Myrtle Jackson, 75 • Rocksey Jackson, 65 • Rosa Jackson, 86 • Royal Jackson, 80 • Russell Jackson, 63 • Nora Jacksn-Daly, 83 • Dorothy Jacques, 87 • Arthur James, Sr, 54 • Geneva James, 98 • Gertie James, 87 • Keith James, 47 • Michael James, 31 • Aleria Jefferson, 69 • Georgia Jenkins, 57 • Joseph Jenkins, 57 • Thomas Jenkins, 64 • Delores Johns, 45 • Lydia Johns, 82 • Althea Johnson, 60 • Gerald Johnson, 34 • Geraldine Johnson, 57 • James Johnson, 47 • John Johnson, 76 • Mabel Johnson, 88 • Mary Johnson, 68 • Preston Johnson, 25 • Willie Johnson, 59 • Anthony Johnston, 96 • Thomas Jolly, 85 • Anthony Jones, 32 • Ella Jones, 80 • Cornelius Jones, Sr, 79 • George Jones, 86 • Vicki Jordan, 38 • Mayola Joseph, 47 • Ruby Joseph, 94 • Malcolm Kafoed, 88 • Salvadore Keelen, 62 • Armstead Keiffer, Sr, 62 • Darryl Keller, 51 • Raymond Keller, 52 • Annie Kelt • John Kelt Sr., 86 • Joey Kennerson, 13 • John Kessner, 60 • Shelton Kinard, 55 • Nathaniel Kingston, 83 • Gretta Kinsey, 61 • Iris Knight, 76 • Jimmie Knight, 75 • Mildred Kramer, 85 • Claris Krause, 87 • Edith Krennerich, 84 • Peter Kuyt, 75 • Carmen Labanca, 95 • Danie LaBasse, 78 • Mary Labat, 84 • John LaCarbiere, 46 • Clifton Lachney, 71 • Jeffrey Lachney, 28 • Althea LaCoste, 73 • Ronald Laddin, 64 • James Lafayette, 97 • Merle Lagasse, 76 • Albertine Lainez, 86 • Athea Lala, 76 • Mike Lala, 74 • Carla Landry, 44 • Lilitha Landry-Prevost, 39 • Muronda Landry, 34 • Neomi Landry, 78 • Lurnice LaRive, 83 • Leroy LaRive, 85 • Elvera Larmeu, 84 • Helen Larre, 91 • Cynthia Lastie, 48 • Marie Latino, 20 • Mathilde Laudumiey, 55 • John Laur, 85 • Willie Lawrence, 47 • Wesley Lawrence, 49 • Gladys Leblanc, 89 • Julia LeBourgeois, 75 • Simon Lee, 88 • Carl Levasseur, 49 • Doneika Lewis, 14 • Nicole Lewis, 36 • Patricia Lewis, 53 • Rickie Lewis, 53 • Mary Lind, 91 • Dominique Liuzza, 53 • James Long, 56 • Mary Lonon, 87 • Frank Lopez, 60 • Todd Lopez, 42 • Shirley Lott, 93 • Edmund Louper, 75 • Harry Louros, 90 • Herbie Love, Sr, 35 • Martha Lozes, 85 • Gregory Lucas, 48 • Linda Lurie, 72 • Elizabeth Lynch, 87 • Leola Lyons, 71 • Ronald Madison, 40 • Peggy Mahaney, 74 • Frankie Major, 47 • Joseph Major, 78 • Mary Mancuso, 87 • Jacqueline Manuel, 65 • Willia Marcellas, 90 • Shirley Mares, 81 • Louise Maurino, 45 • George Marks, 74 • Edna Marsala, 95 • John Marshall, Jr, 66 • Cecile Martin, 95 • Mary Martin, 68 • Plummie Martin, 92 • Willie Martinez, 84 • August Martinolich, 68 • Joyce Masino, 82 • Arthur Mason, 88 • Rendy Matthews, 86 • Jessie May, 79 • Irvin Mayfield, 64 • Lee Mayfield, 41 • Paul McCaddy, 69 • William McCray, 71 • Matthew McDonald, 41 • Joyce McGuire, 77 • Wilda McManus, 70 • Darrell McWilliams, 48 • Lidia Mejia, 14 • Ethe

Melancon, 90 • Lucille Melerine, 85 • Earl Meyer, 80 • Helen Meyer, 79 • Shirley Meyer, 83 • Ro███gliore, 80 • George Milanez, 59 • Arthur Miller, Sr., 78 • Willie Miller, 82 • Darryl Milt███████n Montalbano, 85 • Mary Moore, 64 • Edward Mora, 56 • Laureta Morales, 92 • Robert Morang, 70 • Mary Morant, 52 • Ned Moreland, 81 • Curtis Morrow, 60 • Helen Mortellaro, 83 • Veola Mosby, 79 • Stephen Mosgrove, 60 • Roy Moss, 55 • Matthew Muhoberac, 79 • Matilda Mullen, 78 • Joel Mumphrey, 76 • Johnathan Muse, 18 • William Napol█ 60 • Frances Navis, 80 • Michael Neely, 52 • Elaine Nelson, 90 • Ashley Nettles, 10 ███ Nicholas, 83 • Edward Nora, 66 • Olga Northon, 92 • Mary Norwood, 71 • Fabio███nnor, 85 • Helen Olivier, 82 • Mary Olsen, 78 • Louis Orduna, 90 • Bernadine Owney███Maria Pace, 79 • George Parker, 56 • Janet Parker, 88 • Margaret Parker, 62 • Rose█████er, 83 • Carol Ann Parr, 59 • Norman Parr, 69 • George Perkins, 78 • Peter Pelitere ███Yvette Pereira, 54 • Helen Perret, 90 • Jerry Peters, 64 • Reynette Peters, 87 • Virgin█ █yton, 68 • Beverly Phillips, 65 • Winston Phillips, 81 • Dorothy Pichon, 76 • Ernest Pierre 68 • Juanita Pierre, 69 • Thelma Pinkney, 76 • Rosemary Pino, 83 • Louise Plat█ 53 ██le Poissenot, 89 • Helen Poladura, 86 • Rachel Polmer, 64 • Marvin Ponseti, 75 ███iam Porter, 75 • Leon Preston, 70 • Douglas Price, 43 • Julius Price, 22 • Joseph Prima, 86 • Jerome Prusinski, 86 • Glenn Rambo, 34 • Gladys Randall, 81 • Isaac Randolph, 81 • Verina Ransom, 49 • Janet Rashkin, 80 • Muriel Rasmussen, 90 • Eddie Ray, 59 • Althea Reacord 78 • Olampia Reeves, 87 • Richard Reysack, 81 • Edward Richard, 83 • Sandra Ric████ 8 █ Milton Richards, 62 • LeJohn Richburg, 60 • Jeanne Rickie, 93 • Hugh Ricks, 66 • En███ Riehm, 82 • Clarise Riehms, 75 • Ducky Riess, 92 • Leonard Risper, 74 • Rufus River 77 • Virginia Rizzo, 98 • Rebecca Roark, 61 • Dana Roberts, 43 • Arthur Robertson, 88 • Ethel Robertson, 84 • Edward Robichaux, 61 • John Robichaux, 91 • Virgie Robichaux, 86 • Jean Robin, 78 • Bernice Pizzuto-Robino, 80 • Bessie Robinson, 64 • Pearl Robinson, 82 • Alberto Rocha, 87 • Edgar Rock, 81 • Zola Rodgers, 77 • Eva Rodrigue, 93 • Jos██ odriguez, 78 • Guadalupe Roessler, 79 • Manuel Romero, 84 • Margarita Romero, 88 • Louis Roquevert, 79 • Elizabeth Ross, 55 • Eddie Roy, 63 • Ruth Rulh, 75 • John Russell, 80 • Robert Russell, 37 • Georgia Ryan, 82 • Van Ryan, 84 • Alma Ryburn, 83 • Darlene Saia██ 4 • Antonia Sanfilippo, 79 • Fritz Sauter, 48 • Nicholas Savoca, 75 • Rose Savoie, 91 • Louise Scariano, 88 • Anna Schielder, 75 • Iris Shields, 60 • Cynthi Schiro, 50 • Delores Sch██ 37 • Jake Schiro, Jr., 54 • Catherine Schneider, 81 • Irma Schultz, 76 • John Schultz, 78 • Austin Scott, 66 • Bereita Scott, 87 • Elaine Seeger, 90 • Henry Seifker, 70 • Janie ██████ 93 • Gordon Serou, 67 • Nellie Serpas, 87 • Barbara Sevalia, 55 • Victoria ███████ 93 • Isaac Shanks, 43 • Edna Shannon, 90 • Jerry Shaw, 46 • William Shaw, 82 • Walto█ shepherd, 48 • Lillian Sherman, 92 • Rose Sherman, 88 • Scott Sherman, 54 • Naomi █errod, 84 • Pamela Signal, 41 • Arthur Simmons, 91 • Levie Simmons, Jr., 69 • Richard Simon 53 • Mary Simpson, 60 • Albert Sindibaldi, 87 • Brian Singagliese, 34 • Pauline Singelmann, 84 • Bennie Singleton, 74 • Louise Sires, 93 • Matthew Smallwood, Jr., 52 • Darren Smith, 44 • Elvira Smith, 66 • Freddie Smith, 61 • John Smith, 48 • Lincoln Smith 80 • Marsha Smith, 57 • Ersell Smooth, 33 • Velzie Smith, 84 • Kendra Smooth, 16 • Kendricka Smooth, 18 • Cynthia Snowden, 46 • Edward Sparks, 54 • Susie Sparks, 46 • Jean-██████ Spichiger, 69 • Robert St. Pé, 60 • Henry Stafford, Sr., 63 • Joseph Stafford, 55 • M██y Stafford, 78 • Edward Starks, 58 • Marian Sterns, 56 • Eleanor Stevens, 84 • Charles Stewart, 68 • Karl Stewart, 39 • Onita Stewart, 70 • Marian Stieber, 79 • Raymond Stiebe█ ███etty Stipelcovich, 51 • Nelia Strong, 87 • John Sullivan, 37 • Edith Sutton, 85 • Alvin S███ 68 • Madeline Swiber, 69 • Patricia Sylvester, 50 • Allen Tate, 56 • Herman ait█ 83 • Donald Tappan, 73 • Ronald Taylor, 51 • Tommie Temple, 68 • Emma Thibodeaux Jose█ Teno, 62 • Earl Thomas, 87 • Meddie Thomas, 61 • Rodney Thomas, 82 • Shelly Thoma█ 52 • Michael Thomason, 51 • Donna Thomopolous, 62 • Charles Thompson, 58 • Roy Minnie Thompson, 80 • Lillie Thornton, 99 • Carl Thrift, 57 • Rosalie Tidwell, 83 • Roy Tidwell 82 • Daisy Tobias, 53 • George Torrence, 43 • Alice Toups, 82 • Beulah Toups, 94 • Hong Tran, 71 • Mary Trentecosta, 77 • Ebert Turner, 74 • John Turner, 63 • Meaher Turner 35 • James Ulmer, 70 • Anna Urquhart, 75 • Wendell Valteau, 58 • Aden Varnado, 74 • Wil██ Mae Varnado, 67 • Pamela Vaughn, 53 • Mable Veal, 74 • Lee Venison, 65 • Almeda Verret, 73 • Inez Vidrios, 81 • Mary Wagner, 94 • Shirley Walker, 65 • Willie Walker, 78 • Genevieve Waller, 48 • Rita Warden, 83 • James Warren, 67 • Celina Washington, 70 • James Washington, 60 • Pam Washington, 25 • Rita Washington, 82 • Iretha Watson, 89 • Monroe Watson, 69 • Wilbur Watts, 84 • James Weathers, 29 • Mary Weathersby, 96 • Maurice Weath██ by, 50 • James Weaver, 83 • Phyllis Webster, 60 • Thomas Webster, 77 • Harrison Wesley, 92 • Helen White, 54 • Joan Wickem, 60 • James Wilder, 72 • Audrey Williams, 71 • Clarence Williams, 56 • David Williams, 74 • George Williams, 77 • Joseph Williams, 73 • Lawrence Williams, 56 • Lionel Williams, 49 • Paul Williams, Jr., 60 • Rosetta Williams 9 • Roy Williams, 19 • Walter Williams, 61 • Yolanda Williams, 50 • Madge Wilson, 83 • Art██ Wills Jr., 54 • Raymond Wilson, 63 • Hattie Wimberly, 65 • Alphonse Woods, 77 • Samu██ oods, 72 • Joseph Wright, 89 • Elzie Young, 80 • Gloria Young, 79 • John Young, 44 • Lynus Young, 85 • Robert Young, 85 • Carolyn Youngblood, 42 • Walter Zumpe, 85

COUNTING THE DEAD

IT MAY NEVER BE KNOWN HOW MANY LIVES KATRINA CUT SHORT, BECAUSE THERE ARE BODIES THAT WILL NEVER BE FOUND. And despite the best efforts of forensic pathologists operating at the giant morgue set up at St. Gabriel, outside Baton Rouge, not every corpse could be identified. As of March 1, the official toll of Louisianians killed by Katrina stood at 1,577, a statistic at once horrific and miraculously slight. Based on emergency preparedness drills, FEMA had ordered up 25,000 body bags. For survivors, grief over the disappearance of a loved one was often aggravated by the length of time it took authorities to process the carnage — sometimes months, even when the body had been recovered at home or in familiar circumstances. And still the mysteries endured: men and women whose remains have never been found. Some, it was assumed, had been washed out to sea. Others, experts asserted with equal confidence, had in fact survived but had gone to ground, seeking to escape old lives, debts and entanglements and start fresh. The elderly died in numbers greater than their proportion of the area's population, and so did African-Americans. Many black New Orleanians had come late to homeownership, and many of them lived east of the Industrial Canal, the part of the city that had been last to develop, the part of the city that had been hit hardest by storm surge and floods. The names listed on these pages are those of Katrina's Louisiana casualties who had been positively identified as of March 1, 2006, more than 700 all told.

Peggy Alferez · Betty Arceneaux · Doug Arceneaux · Della Badeaux · Warren Baham · Christina Baham · Joseph Banks · Joan Blackwell · Marjorie Blancher

Nettie Blutcher · Joseph Brossette · Thomas Burke · Benilda Caixeta · Joseph Casamento · Lylton Collins · Amelie Dalier · David Dubuc · Gladys Dupor

A SAMPLING OF PORTRAITS SUGGESTS THE VITALITY, THE VARIETY, THE ENORMITY OF KATRINA'S HUMAN TOLL.

Joseph Brossette's front door wasn't big enough to hold his life story.

Even if it were, the rescue workers scouring the rubble of St. Bernard Parish after Hurricane Katrina had no way of knowing that the 82-year-old Brossette was a native of New Orleans, one of eight children raised in a small house on Urquhart Street. That he served as a paratrooper in World War II, spending much of his tour of duty in the Philippines. That he returned home after the war, married and started a family, living first in the Lower 9th Ward and later in St. Bernard Parish. That he worked for years in the offices of Railway Express Co. That he was an avid bowler who averaged 170 in league games at Imperial Lanes in Chalmette. That he loved to go fishing with his son-in-law down in Delacroix.

So, before moving on to the next address, they recorded on the front door all they knew about the man inside the house on Dauterive Drive. They painted a bright orange X, inlaid with "9/9 0L 1D": September 9, zero living, one dead.

This is how life stories were rendered in post-K New Orleans: strings of hastily rendered letters and numbers, some painted on home fronts, others printed on spreadsheets. Nine months after the storm, the state's official Katrina death toll had reached 1,577; a full accounting of so many lives is simply not possible. Even if you had time to hear all their stories, few hearts could survive the telling.

Easier to talk about demographics (53 percent of storm victims were African-Americans; 53 percent were male; 39 percent were 75 and older) than to talk about 51-year-old Edward "Cool Pop" Sparks, a Regional Transit Authority bus driver who had friends all up and down the St. Claude Avenue line; his 13-year-old son, Edward Jr., who loved basketball and sang in the church choir; his wife, Susie, 46, a Carver Desire Baptist Church volunteer who prepared the Communion table every Saturday; and his Aunt Marjorie Edwards, 85, who rode out the storm at Cool Pop's house on Derby Place because she felt safe there. There was no attic for the four of them to escape to when the water rose to the ceiling.

Less painful to take the Louisiana Department of Health and Hospitals' official list of "Deceased Katrina Victims Released to Families" and skim a random line — Dupor, Gladys, F (female), A (African-American), 51, Orleans (Parish) — than to imagine Southern University at New Orleans' Miss Freshman 1975, a good-timing, French-speaking, fun-loving Creole known to everyone as "Boo," alone in her Gentilly home when the

Doneika Lewis · Cecile Martin · Joyce McGuire · Darryl Milton · Matthew Muhoberac · Olga Northon · Peter Pelitere Jr. · Thelma Pinkney · Sandra Richard

Hugh Ricks · Ducky Riess · Edward Robichaux · John Robichaux · Virgie Robichaux · Manuel Romero · Margarita Romero · Iris Shields · Mary Simpson

Clementine Eleby

Louis Evans Jr.

George Falley

Shirley Mae Falley

Maxine Frischhertz

Eddie Gabriel

Arthur Ginart

Goldie Gulledge

Kendrick Hill

Gary Hingle

Royal Jackson

Annie Kelt

John Kelt Sr.

Cliff Lachney

Althea Lala

Mike Lala

Leroy LaRive

Lurnice LaRive

London Avenue Canal floodwall breached.

"Like a lot of other people, she didn't want to leave," her sister Shirley D. Carriere said. "She thought it was going to be fine."

They all thought it was going to be fine. Many who stayed behind had survived Hurricane Betsy in 1965 and feared no storm that came after. Others dreaded the evacuation more than the storm itself. Others were simply too young to know better, or to imagine worse.

Pam Washington, a 25-year-old single mom who had recently completed her GED and enrolled in the University of New Orleans, sent her daughter away with relatives but stayed home with her 28-year-old boyfriend, Darryl Milton. Not in her wildest nightmares could she have envisioned a storm surge powerful enough to deposit a barge on top of her house with the two of them inside.

Gary Hingle — "Peepaw" to his grandkids — was a Carnival krewe captain who worked as hard on his home in Slidell as he did on cars at the body shop he owned in New Orleans. No way was he leaving the sunroom he and his son Eric had just finished building. The odds of a tree falling on that very sunroom, with him inside, surely seemed much more remote then than they would now.

And the list goes on.

The Rev. Royal Jackson of the Second Highway Baptist Church in Marrero and Elizabeth, his wife of 62 years, had seven children, 19 grandchildren and 29 great-grandchildren. His eastern New Orleans house took on 9 feet of water. Their remains, separated by the floodwaters, were discovered weeks apart.

And on.

Joyce McGuire was a flamboyant businesswoman — first at Sears, then Frederick's of Hollywood, then Carpets by Joyce, her own Chalmette store — who rarely missed a Saints game or turned down an invitation to a Carnival ball. She weathered Katrina in her two-bedroom Arabi home with her son, James Pitre, who left her briefly in a rescue boat to help a stranded neighbor. By the time he returned, she was dead of a heart attack.

And on.

Ersell Smooth was a hotel housekeeper who dreamed of opening her own child-care center. Her three teen-age nieces Kendra, Kendricka and Doneika followed her everywhere — including, on Aug. 28, to her house on Flood Street. As water filled the kitchen, they tried to make their way outside, but none of the four knew how to swim.

And on.

For many families, the loss of life was accompanied by a kind of loss of death. So many loved ones perished alone, their remains unidentified for days or weeks or months, that survivors can only imagine the details of their final hours. For some, there is torment in not knowing; for others, comfort.

Ninety-two-year-old Olga Northon was found six weeks after the storm lying on the floor of her Gentilly home near the piano she once taught neighborhood children to play.

"She was a gracious, kind, dignified lady," said her good friend Leila Haydel. "I'd like to think that as the storm approached, she played the piano for a while, then just went to sleep."

– Mark Lorando, Times-Picayune Assistant Living Editor

rsell Smooth

Kendra Smooth

Kendricka Smooth

Cynthia Snowden

Edward Sparks

Jean-Robert Spichiger

Robert St. Pé

Rodney Thomas Jr.

Roy Tidwell

osalie Tidwell

Mary Ann Trentecosta

Meaher Turner

Pam Washington

Lawrence Ray Williams

Paul Williams Jr.

Arthur Wills Jr.

Walter Zumpe

The Times-Picayune
KATRINA
THE RUIN AND RECOVERY OF NEW ORLEANS

Designed by George Berke

Edited by Jed Horne

Photo editor: Doug Parker

Graphics: Dan Swenson, Lynette Johnson

Copy editors: Patrick Davis, Paula Devlin, Richard Russell

Research: Brent Hightower

Contributing writers: Trymaine Lee, Mark Lorando, Gordon Russell

Photographers: Kathy Anderson, Alex Brandon, Chuck Cook,
Rusty Costanza, Michael DeMocker, Brett Duke, Sean Gardner, Chris Granger,
David Grunfeld, Ted Jackson, Eliot Kamenitz, Ellis Lucia, John McCusker, Cara Owsley,
Susan Poag, Matt Rose, Donald Stout, Scott Threlkeld, Jennifer Zdon

Assistant photo editors: G. Andrew Boyd, Dinah Rogers, Robert Steiner

Photo imaging: Joseph Graham, Alexander Maillho

Layout: Tiffany Bennett Leashore

Dan Shea, Managing Editor/News